50
Beautifully Sweet
Platters and Boards
for Family, Friends,
Holidays, and
Any Occasion

Dessert Boards

Kellie Hemmerly

Creator of *The Suburban Soapbox*

HARVARD COMMON PRESS

Brimming with creative inspiration, how-to projects, and useful information to enrich your everyday life, Quarto Knows is a favorite destination for those pursuing their interests and passions. Visit our site and dig deeper with our books into your area of interest: Quarto Creates, Quarto Cooks, Quarto Homes, Quarto Lives, Quarto Drives, Quarto Explores, Quarto Gifts, or Quarto Kids.

First Published in 2021 by The Harvard Common Press, an imprint of The Quarto Group, 100 Cummings Center, Suite 265-D, Beverly, MA 01915, USA.
T (978) 282-9590 F (978) 283-2742 QuartoKnows.com

The Harvard Common Press titles are also available at discount for retail, wholesale, promotional, and bulk purchase. For details, contact the Special Sales Manager by email at specialsales@quarto.com or by mail at The Quarto Group, Attn: Special Sales Manager, 100 Cummings Center, Suite 265-D, Beverly, MA 01915, USA.

25 24 23 22 21   2 3 4 5

ISBN: 978-0-76037-283-8

Digital edition published in 2021
eISBN: 978-0-76037-284-5

Library of Congress Control Number: 2021940924

Design: Cindy Samargia Laun
Photography: Corinne Hunsicker

Printed in China

Dedication

To my family, Chris, Katie, and Landon,
for enduring the sugar highs and lows during
a weirdly unique year. Thank you for supporting
me while I dreamed of parties, people,
and new celebrations.

Contents

Introduction:
SWEET BEAUTY ON A BOARD

There's not a party or gathering around these days that doesn't have a cheese or charcuterie board present and prominently placed on the buffet table. Grazing around a snack board during a social event is an easy way to catch up with friends and family, but what if you're a sweet tooth, like me.

What if . . . your life revolves around cookies, cake, pastry, and candy? What if . . . at every party you would rather serve up sweet treats instead of savory snacks?

What if . . . you serve up your favorite desserts on a beautiful board or platter? Well, I'm here to tell you that's how sweet dreams are made.

Dessert boards are the perfect way to extend the love of grazing boards to the sweet side. They can be scaled up or down to accommodate any size gathering, and they're fantastic for having a little something to please everyone.

With the boom of snack boards and charcuterie in homes and restaurants over the past few years, the dessert board was just destined to happen. What could be better than a big board loaded with buttery croissants, jam, chocolate cake, decadent truffles, or rich crème brûlée. So, hop on the dessert train and bring this new trend right into your home.

Dessert Boards is a must-have guide to helping you build beautifully arranged happy endings for your own gatherings. From breakfast to midnight, there's a dessert board for every time of day and occasion. Dessert for two or dessert for twenty, you can build a stunning and impressive display on your favorite board or platter. It's basically a blank slate for your own imagination, and you barely have to cook or bake a thing.

Your favorite bakery can be your best friend when it comes to creating a sweet spread to serve your loved ones, or make a quick stop by the local donut shop to load up on your favorites. Most of these easy boards are made with ingredients and snacks you can easily find at a well-stocked grocery store or specialty store. So, even if you're not a culinary wizard, you can easily wow the socks off any party guest with an epic dessert board.

So, here's to sweet celebrations. Enjoy!

THE BLOCKS: WHAT YOU NEED TO BUILD A DESSERT BOARD

Like any building, you need to have a solid foundation on which to build. Selecting the base for your dessert board is simple, but you do need to consider a few factors. Size, material, and type of board can all be determined fairly easily once you know which type of dessert board you want to create. Round boards, rectangular platters, wood trays, and marble slabs are all readily available at many kitchen and housewares stores, but there are a few things to know before purchasing a board.

The Surface

Wood Boards
Wood boards are plentiful, and you can even look in your own kitchen for a wood cutting board that can double as a surface for your dessert board. That's the ultimate multitasker, and it is a great option for people with smaller kitchens where storage space is at a premium.

You can find a variety of wood boards made of maple, walnut, oak, and olive with a natural beauty and great variation in the wood grain. There are also wood boards that are painted with a food-safe coating in a variety of colors and add some pop to your dessert display.

Wood boards are fairly easy to care for: Choose wood with a food-safe finish and a nonporous surface so it doesn't absorb flavors or odor easily. They can be easily cleaned with dish soap and water after each use. Dry thoroughly before storing.

Slate and Marble or Other Stone Slabs
Classic cheese and charcuterie boards are commonly arranged on slate, marble, and other stone boards, and they work equally well for dessert boards.

Slate is easy to find and lightweight, and food displays beautifully against the dark surface. It's also fairly inexpensive and can be written on with chalk to label the items arranged on the board. The only drawback to slate is it can chip or scratch easily. But you can always cover a scratch with a slice of cake.

Marble pastry boards are, like the wood cutting board, an excellent multitasking item in the kitchen. They look stunning as a dessert board surface. They also stay cool, making them a great choice for sweets such as chocolates or puddings. Granite and stone work the same way, staying cool for a longer period of time.

The downsides of stone, marble, and granite are they're heavy and can stain easily. Food items that stain can be placed on a plate before displaying them, or arrange them on a paper doily to protect the surface of your board.

Metal and Wood Trays

Trays, either metal or wooden, are great ways to create dessert boards that need a little containment, like the Movie Night Board (page 126). You can fill them to the rim with loose items that would otherwise fall off the board. Trays are easy to find just about anywhere, and they are easy to care for.

Ceramics

Look around your kitchen, and I promise you probably have a ceramic platter or tray that could double as a dessert board surface. Ceramic is amazing because it washes easily and does not hold odors or stains. They can be heavy and could chip or break if not handled with care.

Once you select your surface, now you need to think about your other tools and accessories, such as tasting forks, spoons, knives, bowls, serving utensils, and mini plates.

The Props

You don't need additional props for your board, but you will need serving utensils so your guests can easily pick up their sweet treats. So, this list is merely a guide to help you build a beautiful board.

Small Bowls and Ramekins

I like to have a variety of small bowls and ramekins on hand to contain smaller items and liquids, similar to what you would use on a cheeseboard. They look more uniform when serving jams, jelly, honey, or smaller ingredients, such as sprinkles or chopped nuts.

I buy white ceramic bowls and dishes so there's never a worry about trying to keep the colors from clashing, and white can be used universally for other kitchen tasks and entertaining. It looks more put together and professional than just putting a jar of jam on the board. Plus, you can never have too many small white bowls and dishes.

If you run out of dishes, break out your favorite cookie cutters. Fun shapes can add a festive vibe to your board. Just don't fill your cookie cutters with liquid because it will seep out the bottom.

Utensils

Small forks, mini spoons, knives, cake servers, ice cream scoops . . . these are all necessities for many dessert boards. Just be sure to decide the type of board you want to create to determine the utensils and serving tools you'll need.

You can purchase disposable utensils at any grocery or party supply store these days, keeping dishes to a minimum. That's perfect party planning right there. Or you can use heirloom utensils, fancy silverware, trendy tapas forks . . . . There's no limit to what you can find to make your board uniquely yours.

THE BUILD: HOW TO BUILD A DESSERT BOARD

Most boards in this book lay out the basic framework for building each type of board. But there are a few guidelines to follow when building any board—sweet or savory.

Start with the big items first. Any bowls or large items, such as cakes, cookies, or cupcakes, should be arranged first. Whatever item is the largest gets placed on the surface so there's no worrying about fitting it on the board after all the items are arranged.

Fill in any large holes with the medium-size items. For example, if your large item is a cake, add the items that are slightly smaller but still need a decent amount of real estate on the surface.

Any empty spaces and gaps can now be filled in with the smaller items, such as jelly beans, candy-coated chocolates, or gummy candies.

Rules are made to be broken, and there are a few instances when I don't follow these directions. As long as you create a focal point on the board and build around it, you will be rewarded with a stunning and perfectly balanced dessert board.

How to Transport a Board

If you're building a board at home and are taking it to a party, you will need to wrap it up. Dessert boards are tricky because cakes or cupcakes are usually frosted and can smear during transit. For those boards, it's best to build them on location.

For boards that are not as complicated or delicate, spread sheets of plastic wrap big enough to wrap up and over the board on a large countertop. Place the board on the plastic wrap and fold the plastic wrap over the board to seal. You can place toothpicks or skewers in any decorated items to keep the plastic wrap from ruining your beautiful work.

Now, let's get building!

1

BOARDS TO

Start the
Day

Coffee Bar BOARD

Serves 6 to 8. Skip the coffeehouse and start the morning with the ultimate coffee bar board. Donuts, biscotti, macaroons, croissants, and scones are just a few of the sweets you can serve your guests. Round it all out with coffee and mix-ins to put a little pep in your step!

INGREDIENTS

Store-Bought Sweets

6 chocolate-dipped biscotti (or your favorite biscotti)

12 waffle cookies

8 pirouette cookies

4 pecan bars

A carafe of coffee

Assorted creamers or nondairy alternatives

Assorted sweeteners, such as sugar, honey, or alternative sweeteners

12 donut holes

12 mini cinnamon rolls

8 mini macaroons

6 mini blueberry scones

2–4 croissants

INSTRUCTIONS

1. I used a small 24-inch (61-cm) wood tray for this board.
2. Arrange the biscotti, waffle cookies, pirouettes, and pecan bars around the outside of the board.
3. Place the coffee, creamer, and sweeteners at the bottom edge of the board or on a separate tray.
4. Fill in the center of the board with clusters of donut holes, cinnamon rolls, macaroons, and scones.
5. Place the croissants in the center of the board and serve.

Note: You can serve the coffee and coffee accoutrements on a separate tray if you're serving a larger crowd.

$\mathit{Light\ and\ Sweet}$ BOARD

Serves 4 to 6. Keep it light, but satisfy your sweet tooth, with this easy board filled with seasonal fruit, chocolate, and chia pudding. It's a great option for the warmer months or to kick off your New Year's resolutions. If you're not a fan of chia pudding, overnight oats are an excellent substitute.

INGREDIENTS

Homemade Treats
Vanilla Chia Seed Pudding
    (page 134) or your favorite
    store-bought chia pudding
1½ cups (144 g) Marshmallow
    Fruit Dip (page 136)

Store-Bought Sweets
4 protein cookies
12 ounces (340 g) superfood
    chocolate bark, broken into
    pieces
2 cups (280 g) fruit-and-nut
    trail mix
2 cups (300 g) assorted fresh
    berries
1 large bunch green grapes
    (approximately 2 cups [300 g])
1 large bunch red grapes
    (approximately 2 cups [300 g])
1 fruit-and-nut cake (8 ounces,
    or 225 g)
3 fruit-and-nut bars, cut into
    1-inch (2.5-cm) pieces
¼ cup (38 g) gooseberries
    (optional)

INSTRUCTIONS

1. I used a 24-inch (61-cm) round board for this arrangement.
2. Divide the chia seed pudding among four small ramekins. You can add more ramekins for a larger crowd or fill smaller shot glasses for another option. Arrange the ramekins down the center of the board.
3. Fill a small bowl with the fruit dip and place it to the lower right of the chia pudding bowls.
4. Fan the cookies to the top right and arrange the chocolate bark below the cookies. Scatter the trail mix below the chocolate bark.
5. Arrange the grapes and nut cake above the dip bowl. Add the fruit-and-nut bar pieces below the bowl, and fill in the remaining spaces with the berries.
6. If using, arrange the gooseberries around the board as a garnish for a pop of color. Add a spoon to the dip bowl for serving.

Notes: Fruit-and-nut cake is a dense cake most often made of figs. It can be found at well-stocked grocery stores in the cheese department. Protein cookies are available at most grocery stores and come in a wide variety of flavors.

Cake for Breakfast BOARD

Serves 8. Eat cake for breakfast! All the breakfast cake you can imagine is on one big board, starting with a pound cake French toast filled with fresh fruit and ending with blueberry coffee cake. This board has something for everyone. Serve it all up with a pitcher of warm maple syrup. You can easily scale this board up or down for any party size by adding more pancakes or an extra coffee cake.

INGREDIENTS

Homemade Treats
Pound Cake French Toast
  (page 133)
Blueberry Pancakes (page 134)
  or your favorite pancake
  recipe

Store-Bought Sweets
2 cups (300 g) assorted fresh
  berries
1 blueberry coffee cake or your
  favorite coffee cake recipe
1 raspberry crumb cake or
  your favorite crumb cake
1½ cups (482 g) maple syrup,
  warmed
Butter, for serving

INSTRUCTIONS

1. I used a 24-inch (61-cm) rectangular platter for serving. You can use a round board or platter. Just be sure it's large enough to hold enough for the party you're serving.
2. Make the pound cake French toast and arrange it in a cake shape at the top corner of the board. Fill the center of the pound cake with mixed berries.
3. Slice the coffee cake into ½-inch (1-cm) slices and arrange it in a "river" diagonally down the center of the board, starting at the opposite corner from the pound cake.
4. Shingle the pancakes along the bottom edge of the coffee cake.
5. Arrange the sliced crumb cake in a group below the pound cake.
6. Fill the remaining areas with fruit. Serve with a small pitcher of syrup and pats of butter.

Note: You can use any flavor pound cake, coffee cake, or pancakes. For a larger group, add a variety of pancake flavors to satisfy everyone.

Teatime BOARD

Serves 4. Tea for two or twenty-two, this teatime-inspired board is easy to modify for an afternoon sweet treat with a friend or a larger gathering, such as a bridal shower or Sunday brunch. Filled with colorful fruit tarts, macarons, scones, and fruit, this fun spread is a cornucopia of sweet treats! Everything I used for this board was store-bought, making it one of the easier dessert boards in this book.

INGREDIENTS

Store-Bought Sweets

2–4 fruit tarts (depending on the size)

12 scones, assorted flavors (we used blueberry and vanilla here)

4–6 madeleines or other soft cookie

4 crispy wafer cookies or pizzelles

8 assorted macarons

Assorted fresh fruit

Tea, cream, and sugar cubes, for serving

INSTRUCTIONS

1. I used a 13-inch (33-cm) rectangular platter for serving.
2. Arrange the fruit tarts on the corners of the board. If using four tarts, place them in each of the four corners.
3. Arrange the scones around the fruit tarts in a shingled pattern.
4. Fill in the remaining spaces with the madeleines and cookies. Setting them on their side provides texture to your board and makes it easier to grab. Fill in the board with assorted fruit.
5. Serve with tea, cream, and sugar cubes.

Note: If you're serving a larger crowd, it's easy to expand the size of the board by adding one fruit tart per guest. Also, increase the number of macarons, allowing for two per guest. Adding an additional flavors of scones also helps build out a bigger board.

Yogurt Parfait BOARD

Serves 12. A healthy start to the day, this fabulously easy yogurt parfait board is an excellent addition to a weekend brunch. Flavored yogurt is the centerpiece of this board, with bowls of granola, fruit, sprinkles, nuts, and chocolate for guests to make their very own yogurt parfait. There's truly something to please even the pickiest guests. Use your favorite flavored yogurt or plain greek yogurt for a variety of options.

INGREDIENTS

Store-Bought Sweets

1 container (35 ounces, or 992 g) vanilla yogurt

1 container (35 ounces, or 992 g) strawberry yogurt

1 cup (175 g) mini dark chocolate chips

1 cup (224 g) mini candy-coated chocolates

1 cup (122 g) granola

1 cup (224 g) pomegranate arils

1 cup (100 g) chopped walnuts

2 bananas, sliced

3 cups (450 g) assorted fresh berries

INSTRUCTIONS

1. I used a 24-inch (61-cm) round marble board for serving.
2. Fill two large bowls with the yogurt and place them in the center of the board with about 6 to 8 inches (15 to 20 cm) in between.
3. Arrange five smaller bowls on the board and fill each with the chocolate chips, candy-coated chocolates, granola, pomegranate arils, and nuts.
4. Fan the banana around two of the side bowls and arrange the remaining fruit on the board in groups. I like to place the strawberries stem side down for uniformity.
5. Top the yogurt bowls with a few fresh berries. Add serving spoons to the yogurt bowls.
6. Serve the board with smaller tasting spoons and glasses for guests to build their parfaits.

Note: To keep your bananas from browning, drizzle them with diluted honey. Simply whisk together 2 tablespoons (28 ml) of water with 1 tablespoon (20 g) honey and drizzle over the banana slices. Lemon works as well, but the honey keeps the bananas sweet instead of adding the tartness of lemon.

Donut Dessert BOARD

Serves 14 to 18. A sweet start to the day! Donuts in every shape and size, filled or not, are piled high for the most delightfully colorful breakfast board ever. Top with a few chocolate-covered strawberries to round out the flavors. The beauty of this board is that you can make it for an informal family breakfast or a large brunch gathering. If you have a favorite donut recipe, this is a fantastic way to showcase it.

INGREDIENTS

Homemade Treats

6 Chocolate-Covered
   Strawberries (page 129)

Store-Bought Sweets

6 assorted frosted donuts

6 assorted filled donuts

6 assorted cinnamon buns or
   morning buns

6 assorted decorated donuts
   (covered in coconut, nuts,
   or sprinkles)

1 dozen assorted mini donuts

2 dozen assorted donut holes

1 pint (312 g) fresh raspberries

1 pint (290 g) fresh blueberries

1 pint (357 g) fresh strawberries

INSTRUCTIONS

1. I used a large 24-inch (61-cm) round board, which is the perfect size for serving 14 to 18 people. You can use a smaller board if you're serving fewer people.
2. Arrange the frosted and filled donuts on the bottom in a single layer.
3. Fill in the large spaces with the cinnamon buns and decorated donuts.
4. Fill in the remaining spaces with the mini donuts and donut holes.
5. Sprinkle the berries around the donuts to fill in the smaller spaces.
6. Top some of the donuts with the chocolate-covered strawberries and serve.

Pastries and Danish Breakfast BOARD

Serves 8 to 10. Sunday smiles are a little bigger when everyone wakes up to a beautiful board filled with buttery pastries, fruit-filled danish, and morning buns. Serve alongside bowls filled with fruit preserves, jams, or butter, then balance it all with fresh berries. It's the perfect companion for your cup of coffee. You can use any combination of pastry you like, and it's easy to size up or down depending on how many guests you're serving.

INGREDIENTS

Homemade Treats
Raspberry Jam (page 137) or your favorite store-bought jam

Store-Bought Sweets
5–6 assorted fruit- or cheese-filled danish

3 plain croissants

3–4 filled croissants

2–4 morning buns or cinnamon rolls

6–8 strawberries

INSTRUCTIONS

1. I used a large 24-inch (61-cm) round board, which is the perfect size for serving 8 to 10 people. You can use a smaller board if you're serving fewer people.
2. Arrange the danish in a straight line down the center of the board.
3. Place one or two small ramekins on the board, with one at the top of the danish line and one at the bottom. Fill each bowl with the jam. If you're serving a smaller crowd, use just one bowl of jam.
4. Add the croissants in groups along the sides of the danish. Fill the remaining spaces with the morning buns or cinnamon rolls.
5. Arrange the strawberries in any open spots on the board.
6. Serve with spoons for spreading the jam on the pastries.

Spring Brunch BOARD

Serves 6. The spring season seems to be the kickoff for brunch season, and I'm here for it with this spring brunch board. Inspired by all the bright, vibrant colors spring has to offer, this sweet board is loaded with beautiful petit fours, chocolate-covered strawberries, fruit tarts, cinnamon rolls, and miniature rounds of Brie. Presented with a bowl of fresh fruit jam to spread on the scones or Brie, this board is always a surprising treat. Serve alongside mimosas or your favorite cold-brew coffee.

INGREDIENTS

Homemade Treats
6–12 Chocolate-Covered Strawberries (page 129)
1 cup (235 ml) Raspberry Jam (page 137) or your favorite store-bought jam

Store-Bought Sweets
3–6 fruit tarts
12 mini scones
12 assorted macarons
6 petit four
12 mini cinnamon rolls
10–12 assorted cookies (stroopwafels, waffle cookies, and cookie straws are great options)
6 mini wheels of Brie
1 cup (160 g) chocolate-covered almonds
Assorted fresh fruit

INSTRUCTIONS

1. I used a 24-inch (61-cm) oval board for serving.
2. Arrange the fruit tarts in a group on one side of the board. If you're making a board for a larger crowd, group the fruit tarts in clusters of three on opposite sides of the board.
3. Place a bowl to the far side of the board and fill with the jam.
4. Arrange the scones in a "river" across the board on a diagonal and arrange the macarons to one side.
5. Group the petit fours on the opposite side of the scone river, and then group the remaining items in the spaces in between.
6. Arrange the fruit in the gaps and serve.

Note: If you're unfamiliar with petit fours, they're a small bite-size confections most often made of cake and covered in a thin layer of frosting or chocolate. They're often beautifully decorated, making them a great addition to any dessert board.

2

BOARDS FOR

Happy Holidays

New Year's Eve BOARD

Serves 16. Ring in the new year the sweetest way possible with the ultimate celebratory treats! A bakery-style cake decorated with a clock that's minutes from the new year is surrounded by champagne gummies, chocolate-covered pretzels, chocolate-dipped cookies, truffles, and more. You can add your own favorite homemade treats or pick up everything at your local store or bakery.

INGREDIENTS

Homemade Treats

12 Chocolate-Covered Pretzels
   (page 136)

Store-Bought Sweets

1 6-inch (15-cm) clockface
   layer cake

12 assorted chocolate truffles

1½ cups (270 g) champagne
   gummy bears

1½ cups (273 g) champagne
   gumdrops

12 mini cupcakes

12 chocolate-dipped assorted
   cookies

12 chocolate cookie straws

Mini chocolate champagne
   bottles

INSTRUCTIONS

1. I used a 24-inch (61-cm) round marble board for serving.
2. Place the cake in the center of the board, making sure 12:00 is facing the top of the board.
3. Arrange the remaining ingredients in clusters or groups around the cake, filling in the spaces to ensure most of the board is covered.
4. You may need to remove the treats from the board before cutting the cake and serving.

Note: Because New Year's is usually a late-night affair, this is a great board to rely on your local bakery or candy store to help you create a showstopper. I also like to use all store-bought items for boards when I'm entertaining a larger group. It's easier to have extra ingredients to replenish the board as needed.

Holiday Cookie BOARD

Serves 12. A holiday cookie board is a must-have during the holiday season, and it's a great way to showcase your favorites. I like to add nostalgic candy, such as peppermint starburst and small jewel-like sweets, because they add extra sparkle. Christmas cookie cutters are a great alternative to bowls for this board, adding festive flair without breaking the bank. The cookies I recommend are a few of our favorites; customize your own board with your own family heirlooms.

INGREDIENTS

Homemade Treats

6–12 Classic Chocolate Chip
   Cookies (page 132)

Store-Bought Sweets

1 cup (227 g) small hard
   candies

6 pizzelle cookies

6 sugar cookie cutouts

6 macaroons

6 rugelach

6 chocolate-covered
   sandwich cookies

6 thumbprint cookies

1 cup (227 g) peppermint
   starburst candies

1 cup (182 g) holiday-inspired
   jelly candies

6 mini candy canes

INSTRUCTIONS

1. I used a 24-inch (61-cm) round board for serving. I like a board with higher sides to keep the cookies and candy contained so you can stuff the board full of holiday goodies.
2. Place the cookie cutter on the board; I like it slightly off center. Fill it with the small candies.
3. Arrange the cookies in groups in a shingled fashion, starting with the largest cookies first. Try to mix up the textures and colors so they're more easily distinguishable.
4. Layer in the more aesthetically pleasing cookies to showcase them on top, then fill in the remaining spaces with candy.

Note: There are no rules to building a holiday cookie board. Branch out by adding your favorite sweets, such as holiday fudge, caramels, or gingerbread.

Fall Harvest BOARD

Serves 6. This is a festive and FUN dessert board that's filled with fall flavor. This Thanksgiving turkey board starts with rows of pumpkin rolls, sandwich cookies, and cupcakes. As with many of the holiday boards, you can make your favorite homemade recipes, but I recommend using mostly store-bought treats to keep holiday entertaining a breeze.

INGREDIENTS

Store-Bought Sweets

½ large pear

1 12-inch (30-cm)-long pumpkin roll

22 chocolate sandwich cookies

14 maple sandwich cookies

13 mini cupcakes decorated with fall colors

8 chocolate florentine or chocolate chip cookies

2 candy eyes (I use frosting to glue them to the pear)

1 small yellow candy for the beak

1 piece (¼ inch, or 6 mm) red licorice

INSTRUCTIONS

1. I used a 24-inch (61-cm) round board for serving.
2. Place the pear, cut-side down, at the bottom of the board with the larger end of the pear facing the edge.
3. Slice the pumpkin roll into ½-inch (1-cm) slices and fan them out around the edge of the board, starting and stopping at the pear.
4. Layer the chocolate sandwich cookies around the inner edge of the pumpkin rolls, then repeat with the maple sandwich cookies.
5. Arrange the cupcakes around the edge of the maple sandwich cookies, then fill the remaining space with the florentines.
6. Make a face on the pear with candy eyes, candy beak, and licorice snood.

Fun fact: Wondering what a snood is? It's the floppy red pouch that hangs from a turkey's beak.

Halloween Jack-o-Lantern BOARD

Serves 10. Create a jack-o-lantern without the carving by creating a sweet and silly pumpkin out of your favorite candy. This is a great board to let the kids take over, because there's no cutting or cooking required. Grab an assortment of orange candy, black licorice for the face, and green jelly candies for the stem . . . and build.

INGREDIENTS

Store-Bought Sweets

2 cups (150 g) jellied orange slices

18 orange licorice twists

1½ cups (525 g) chocolate/caramel kiss candies with an orange wrapper

1½ cups (180 g) orange gummy bears

1½ cups (180 g) orange creamsicle gummy bears

6 pieces black licorice, cut into 1½-inch (3.5-cm) pieces

½ cup (75 g) jellied green spearmint leaves

INSTRUCTIONS

1. I used a 14-inch (36-cm) rectangle slate board for serving.
2. Starting with the orange slices, form the outside edges of the pumpkin.
3. Fill in the pumpkin with even rows of orange licorice, chocolate/caramel candies, and gummy bears.
4. Create a jack-o-lantern face using the black licorice.
5. Using the spearmint leaves, make a stem on top of the pumpkin.

Pick Your Flag Colors Celebration BOARD

Serves 12. Festive and bold, this spread is like a colorful candy explosion on a board. Swirly lollipops, chocolate truffles, licorice, cupcakes, gummy candy, and more make this beautiful dessert platter suitable for so many celebrations. Because I live in the US, I used red, white, and blue, but you can easily substitute M&Ms, jelly beans, candy stars, licorice sticks, and other treats that match the color of your country's flag.

INGREDIENTS

3 star-shaped bowls

1 cup (208 g) red, white, and blue candy-coated chocolates, such as M&Ms

1 cup (160 g) red, white, and blue jelly beans

1 cup (156 g) red, white, and blue candy stars

8 swirl lollipops

9 mini cupcakes

1 cup wrapped chocolate truffle candies

24 red and blue sweet and sour licorice strips

2 cups (225 g) white gum drops

2 cups (225 g) red raspberry gummy candies

1 cup (90 g) white-chocolate–covered pretzels

2 cups (225 g) red licorice swirls

1½ cups (211.5 g) white chocolate Kit Kat Bites

INSTRUCTIONS

1. For this board, I used a 24 inch (61-cm) round wooden tray.
2. Arrange the star bowls down the center of the board.
3. Fill one bowl with the candy-coated chocolate, one bowl with the jelly beans, and the remaining bowl with the star candies.
4. Place the lollipops to the right of the center star bowl in a shingle pattern and then arrange the cupcakes to the left of the star bowl.
5. Fill the space above the lollipops with the chocolate truffles and then below the lollipops stack the sweet and sour licorice strips.
6. Arrange the white gum drops and red gummy candies above the cupcakes. Then, below arrange the red licorice and pretzels.
7. Fill in the remaining spaces with the Kit Kat Bites and serve with tongs, if desired.

Easter Bunny Treats BOARD

Serves 8. Even if the Easter Bunny didn't drop off a basket, you can still enjoy all the sweet treats on this bright, colorful board. Classic marshmallow peeps, bunnies, and ducks are just a few of the sugary confections that will be the first to vanish. Rainbow lollipops, chocolate-covered pretzels, robin eggs, and cupcakes frame the Easter sugar cookies perfectly. Decorate a few chocolate-covered strawberries to look like carrots and don't forget the jelly beans!

INGREDIENTS

Homemade Treats

8 Easter-themed Basic Sugar
  Cookies (page 131)
6 Chocolate-Covered Pretzels
  (page 136)
8 Chocolate-Covered
  Strawberries (page 129)

Store-Bought Sweets

2 cups (320 g) jellybeans
½ cup (60 g) robin eggs candy
6–8 marshmallow Peeps
2 cups (100 g) Easter
  marshmallows (bunnies
  and ducks)
6 Easter egg swirl lollipops
8 chocolate carrots
6 mini Easter cupcakes
¼ cup (45 g) gummy candy
  carrots

INSTRUCTIONS

1. I used a 24-inch (61-cm) round marble board for serving.
2. Position one large bowl and one small bowl on the board.
3. Arrange the sugar cookies in a row down the center of the board in between the two bowls.
4. Fill the larger bowl with the jellybeans and the smaller bowl with the robin eggs.
5. Arrange the pretzels, strawberries, marshmallows, lollipops, chocolate carrots, and cupcakes in groups around the board.
6. Fill in any remaining gaps with the gummy candy carrots.

Note: Add some spring florals, such as bluebells or smaller pansies, to bring a fresh spring flair to your creation. Be sure to use edible varieties, even if you don't plan to eat them.

Lucky Leprechaun BOARD

Serves 8. St. Patrick's Day has never been sweeter than with this festive dessert board. It's loaded with rainbow lollipops, rainbow ribbons, chocolate sandwich cookies, green starburst candies, cupcakes, pretzels, and more gold than a leprechaun could wish for. This board is easily scaled up or down depending on the size of your gathering.

INGREDIENTS

Semi-Homemade Sweets

12 Chocolate-Covered Pretzels (page 136)

6–8 rainbow candy Crispy Cereal Treats (page 130)

Store-Bought Sweets

16 ounces (455 g) gold foil chocolate coins

3–6 large rainbow swirl lollipops

24 mint chocolate sandwich cookies

1½ cups (340 g) green starburst candies

16 rainbow belts

6–8 mini cupcakes with green and white sprinkles

8 ounces (225 g) mini rainbow candy-coated chocolate candies

INSTRUCTIONS

1. I used a 24-inch (61-cm) round board for serving.
2. Make two small piles of the gold coins at the top and bottom of the board.
3. Arrange the pretzels in a row down the center of the board to "connect" the two gold piles (like a pretzel rainbow of sorts).
4. Arrange the lollipops in a stack on one side of the coins, then position the sandwich cookies in a row on their sides so the green is visible.
5. Scatter the green starburst candies next to the sandwich cookies; this will keep the cookies from rolling away.
6. Arrange the rainbow belts on the opposite side of the board from the lollipops, then place the crispy cereal treats to the right of the belts.
7. Place the cupcakes at the bottom of the board, then scatter the chocolate candies to the left of the cupcakes.

Note: You can fill the board out more and even add more color by filling in the gaps with more rainbow-colored chocolate candies.

Valentine Sweetheart BOARD

Serves 12. Sweets for your sweetheart or your favorite galentines, this valentine dessert board is loaded with all things sweet, tart, hot, and rich. Everything you want in the love of your life, right? Bakeries are filled with heart-shaped confections right around the holiday, so this arrangement is easy to make with mostly store-bought ingredients. We use a heart-shaped cookie cutter as a bowl to contain some of the smaller candies—and it's super cute, too! This board is easily scaled down for a more intimate gathering.

INGREDIENTS

Homemade Treats
6–12 Chocolate-Covered Pretzels (page 136)

Store-Bought Sweets
1 6-inch (15-cm) heart-shaped chocolate cake

1 cup (182 g) valentine gummy candy

6 valentine sugar cookies

14 mini cupcakes

1 cup (224 g) mini sweet tart hearts

1 cup (120 g) mini gummy candy hearts

8–10 chocolate nonpareils

5–6 foil-wrapped chocolate hearts

INSTRUCTIONS

1. I used a 24-inch (61-cm) heart-shaped board for serving. A round or oval board would work well, too.
2. Place the heart-shaped cake on the left side of the board and position the cookie cutter on the right. Fill the cookie cutter with the valentine gummy candy.
3. Arrange the cookies in a row from top to bottom to the right of the cake, then repeat the pattern with the cupcakes.
4. Stack a few pretzels on the board to the right of the cupcakes.
5. Arrange the remaining candies in the open spaces on the board.
6. Serve with champagne for a real celebration of love!

3

Around
the World

BOARDS

Sushi and Sweets BOARD

Serves 12. Take a trip to the East with an Asian-inspired sweets board complete with gummy candy sushi, mochi, Chocorooms, Pocky, chocolate pandas, and mini mochi. This board is so fun to make, and I like to separate the sushi from the "sweets" for a more realistic sushi spread. Kids and adults alike love this unique dessert board. If you have a favorite mochi recipe, this is a great way to showcase it. I saved time by purchasing all my ingredients at a specialty candy store, but you can also find everything at an online candy retailer.

INGREDIENTS

Store-Bought Sweets

Assorted candy sushi

Assorted mochi (chocolate, strawberry, and matcha are used here)

1 package (5 ounces, or 142 g) strawberry mini mochi candy

1 box (2.4 ounces, or 68 g) strawberry Pocky

1 box (2.4 ounces, or 68 g) chocolate Pocky

2 boxes (5 ounces, or 142 g each) Chocorooms

2 packages (2 ounce, or 57 g each) Hello Panda choco cream biscuits

INSTRUCTIONS

1. I used one 12-inch (30-cm) square platter and one 13-inch (33-cm) long platter. You can use one large platter if you prefer.
2. Arrange the sushi candy and larger mochi on a platter in a precise pattern, similar to what you would find in a sushi restaurant.
3. On the second platter, arrange the mini mochi down the center of the platter and fan out the Pocky on each side.
4. Scatter the Chocorooms and the pandas in the remaining spaces of the board.

Note: What's mochi? Mochi is a Japanese rice cake made of a short-grain Japonica glutinous rice (called mochigome) and water, sugar, and cornstarch. The rice is pounded into a paste before being molded into shapes. It's smooth and chewy, often flavored with chocolate, strawberry, mango, lychee, and matcha.

Dessert Nacho BOARD

Serves 6. Sugar, spice, and everything nice . . . that's what these nachos are made of. Loaded dessert nachos are piled high with chopped strawberries, kiwi fruit, nuts, bananas, coconut, and whipped topping. Drizzled with chocolate and caramel sauce, these nachos are always gone in a flash. What's even better, the nachos are made with tortillas fried until crispy and sprinkled with cinnamon-sugar.

INGREDIENTS

Homemade Treats
24 Cinnamon-Sugar
  Tortilla Chips (page 135)

Store-Bought Sweets
1 pint (357 g) strawberries,
  washed, hulled, and
  chopped
3 kiwi fruit, peeled and
  chopped
1 banana, peeled and
  thinly sliced
½ cup (40 g) shredded
  sweetened coconut
¼ cup (30 g) chopped walnuts
¾ cup (45 g) whipped topping
¼ cup (60 ml) chocolate sauce
¼ cup (60 ml) caramel sauce
½ cup (56 g) fresh red
  currants (optional)

INSTRUCTIONS

1. I used a 14-inch (36-cm) ceramic platter for this board.
2. Fill the board with half the tortilla chips. Top with half the strawberries, kiwi fruit, banana, coconut, and walnuts.
3. Add the remaining tortilla chips to the top of the pile and sprinkle with the remaining fruit, coconut, and nuts.
4. Add the whipped topping. Drizzle with both the chocolate and caramel sauces.
5. Add fresh currants for a garnish, if desired.

Note: Tortilla chips can be made up to 24 hours in advance. For best results, warm them in the oven for 10 minutes before assembling your nacho board and serve immediately.

Molto Dolce BOARD
(ITALIAN SWEETS BOARD)

Serves 12. Italian classics are the heroes of the very popular molto dolce board. Molto dolce means "very sweet" in Italian, and it perfectly explains everything arranged on this gorgeous display. Mini cannoli, biscotti, pizzelle, Italian cookies, tiramisu, and sfogliatella are perfect morning, noon, or night. And don't forget the Italian rainbow cookies. They add a pop of color and are always the first to vanish. You can also purchase one or two servings of tiramisu from your favorite Italian restaurant and cut it into bite-size pieces—a great way to ensure everyone gets a taste of every Italian morsel.

INGREDIENTS
Store-Bought Sweets
24 pizzelle cookies (chocolate or vanilla, or both)

12 mini cannoli

12 bite-size pieces of tiramisu

6 sfogliatella

12 mini biscotti

12 Italian rainbow cookies

12 assorted Italian cookies

Coffee, tea, or dessert wine, for serving

INSTRUCTIONS
1. I used a 24-inch (61-cm) rectangular board for serving.
2. Start with the largest desserts first. Arrange the pizzelle, cannoli, tiramisu, and sfogliatella on the board in small groups. You may not need to use all of the ingredients; save the remaining in the kitchen to replenish the board as needed.
3. Fill the remaining spaces on the board with the biscotti, rainbow cookies, and Italian cookies.
4. Serve with coffee, tea, or dessert wine.

Note: Because some of the ingredients are best served chilled, this board should be served soon after assembling.

Gâterie Sucrée BOARD
(SWEET TREAT BOARD)

Serves 8. French pastries are an art form, and this board is loaded with all the gâterie sucrée (sweet treats) you would imagine finding in France. From simple apple tarts to a delightfully layered opera cake, a French pastry shop is your one-stop shop for every morsel you'll need to build this stunning board. If you're a macaron maven or love to craft colorful petit fours, this is the board to showcase your talents. If you're like me, find your favorite pastry shop and build your board with whatever catches your eye.

INGREDIENTS

Store-Bought Sweets

2 fruit tarts

2 opera cakes

2 fruit mousse cakes

2 chocolate mousse cakes

10 assorted macarons

8 petit fours

2 chocolate éclairs

Assorted chocolates

INSTRUCTIONS

1. I used two 24-inch (61-cm) rectangular tapas boards for serving.
2. Starting with the larger items, arrange the tarts, opera cakes, and mousse cakes on the board first in a zigzag pattern.
3. Position the macarons, petit fours, and éclairs in between the cakes, setting some of the macrons on their side.
4. Fill the remaining spaces with the assorted chocolates.

Note: If you prefer your boards to be filled out a little more, you can add more macarons, chocolates, or even fruit. When working with delicate tarts, pies, and cakes, I prefer to leave more space on the board for easier serving.

4

Family Friendly

BOARDS

Caramel Apple Dipping BOARD

Serves 8. Caramel apples are a fall favorite, and we scaled them down a bit for less mess—and less waste! Sure, you can make one whole caramel apple, but they're difficult to eat. We cut the apples into wedges, added a skewer, and made a board that's a total hit with kids of any age. This board is easily scalable for crowds large or small, and the topping ideas are limitless. The board here is perfectly sized for a fun after-school snack, but you can make this on a much larger board with additional dipping options for a Halloween party or fall get-together.

INGREDIENTS

Store-Bought Sweets

4 apples, cored and cut into wedges

12 skewers

1 cup (235 ml) caramel sauce

¼ cup (52 g) candy-coated chocolates

¼ cup (30 g) chopped walnuts

¼ cup (48 g) rainbow sprinkles

3 whole caramel apples, optional

INSTRUCTIONS

1. I used a 24-inch (61-cm) rectangular board for serving.
2. Insert a skewer into the end of each apple wedge and set aside.
3. Arrange a medium-size ramekin and three small ramekins on the board.
4. Fill the medium ramekin with the caramel sauce and the small ramekins with the chocolates, walnuts, and sprinkles.
5. Arrange the apple wedges and the caramel apples, if using, on the board for dipping.
6. Serve immediately.

Note: To keep your apple wedges from browning, dip each wedge into a mixture of 2 parts water to 1 part honey for a few seconds. The honey will keep the apples from browning without adding the tartness of lemon juice, which is a common ingredient used to prevent browning.

Try these dipping options:

- Mini chocolate chips
- Nonpareils
- Red Hots
- Chopped toffee bits
- Shredded coconut
- White chocolate chips
- Melted chocolate
- Mini marshmallows

Carnival Treats BOARD

Serves 10. Summer fairs and carnivals are busting at the seams with sweet treats—so I put them all on one board for a taste of fair food favorites. Funnel cakes, caramel apples, cotton candy, and more are all in one spot for a sweet summer celebration. You can even add savory favorites such as corn dogs and soft pretzels to mix things up. I purchased many of the ingredients at the store, but you can easily substitute with your favorite homemade recipes.

INGREDIENTS

Homemade Treats
6–8 Funnel Cakes (page 135)
Powdered sugar, for dusting

Store-Bought Sweets
4 cups (47 g) cotton candy
6–8 mini hand pies
8–10 rainbow swirl lollipops
   (both round and long)
2 pounds (907 g) assorted
   fudge
3–6 caramel apples

INSTRUCTIONS

1. I used a 24-inch (61-cm) round board for serving.
2. Arrange the cotton candy in a line down the center of the board, being sure to fluff it up.
3. Place the funnel cakes on the left of the cotton candy and dust with powdered sugar.
4. Position the hand pies below the funnel cakes and slip some longer lollipops in between the funnel cakes and pies to add some color and division between the two items.
5. Place three round lollipops at the top of the board and three round lollipops at the bottom of the board.
6. Shingle the fudge slices directly across from the hand pies, and arrange the caramel apples in the remaining space.
7. Serve immediately.

Note: This board is best served soon after the funnel cakes are fried. You can top each funnel cake with your favorite pie filling, chocolate sauce, or fresh fruit to add more flair.

Beach Boardwalk
Sweets BOARD

Serves 10. You don't need to trek to the beach to enjoy your favorite boardwalk snacks. This beach boardwalk sweets board is packed with the best of the boards. Sweet, rich fudge, colorful saltwater taffy, funnel cakes, caramel corn, and fluffy cotton candy play perfectly on a big, round board. We love serving this at pool parties when we can't get to the coast, but it's also fun in the winter when you need a taste of summer. Add a few gummy candy sharks and whales for added color and sea life.

INGREDIENTS

Homemade Treats
6–8 Funnel Cakes (page 135)
Powdered sugar, for dusting

Store-Bought Sweets
3 pounds (1.4 kg) saltwater taffy
4 cups (171 g) caramel corn
¼ pound (115 g) gummy candy sharks and whales (optional)
2 pounds (907 g) assorted fudge
4 cups (47 g) cotton candy

INSTRUCTIONS

1. I used a 24-inch (61-cm) round board for serving.
2. Arrange the saltwater taffy in a line down the center of the board.
3. Place the funnel cakes on the left of the taffy and dust with powdered sugar.
4. Add a pile of caramel corn right below the funnel cakes and arrange a few gummy candies around the funnel cakes to break up the color a bit.
5. Shingle the fudge slices directly across from the funnel cakes and cotton candy in the remaining space, fluffing it up a bit.
6. Serve immediately.

Note: This board is best served soon after the funnel cakes are fried. You can top each funnel cake with your favorite pie filling, chocolate sauce, or ice cream!

Cupcake Decorating
BOARD

Serves 10. A party just isn't a party without cupcakes, and this cupcake decorating board ensures everyone gets their cupcake just as they like it. Naked cupcakes are served up with piping bags filled with frosting, sprinkles, candy, and cookies so party guests can all have their cake and eat it, too! I purchased cupcakes ready-made at the grocery store and asked for them unfrosted, making this board one of the easiest ever to put together. Store-bought frosting is also a huge time-saver, but you can make your favorite homemade cupcakes and frosting if you prefer.

INGREDIENTS

Store-Bought Sweets

1 cup (192 g) rainbow sprinkles

1 cup (192 g) candy-coated chocolate sprinkles

1 cup (192 g) sweet tart sprinkles

10 assorted cupcakes, unfrosted

1 cup (22 g) Swedish Fish

1 cup (150 g) mini chocolate chip cookies

1 cup (144 g) mini chocolate sandwich cookies

1 cup (120 g) assorted gumballs

2 cups (250 g) chocolate frosting

2 cups (250 g) vanilla frosting

2 cups (250 g) strawberry frosting

INSTRUCTIONS

1. I used a 24-inch (61-cm) rectangular platter for serving.
2. Arrange three bowls in the center of the board and fill each with one type of sprinkles.
3. Arrange the cupcakes on each side of the board.
4. Fill the spaces in between the bowls with the swedish fish, cookies, and gumballs.
5. Fill a pastry bag fitted with a decorating tip with the chocolate frosting. Fill an additional 2 pastry bags with the vanilla and strawberry frosting.
6. Place the pastry bags on the edges of the platter and serve.

Note: You can make a larger platter for a bigger crowd and add more cupcakes as needed. Be sure to increase the amount of sprinkles or add additional options, such as mini chocolate chips, caramel sauce, shredded coconut, or chopped nuts, so there's plenty for everyone.

Ice Cream Sandwich BOARD

Serves 6. Ice cream sandwiches are a staple of summer, so why not serve them up on a beautiful board? This board is jam packed with the BEST ice cream sandwiches . . . from the classic chocolate and vanilla to the most over-the-top cookie sandwiches. You can make your own with your favorite cookie recipe or just buy a variety for one epic summer dessert board. I even added a few cookie dough and brownie batter bites as a little sweet treat for those guests who don't want to indulge in a whole sandwich.

INGREDIENTS

Store-Bought Sweets

6–8 assorted cookie ice cream sandwiches

6–8 assorted brownie ice cream sandwiches

3–6 regular ice cream sandwiches

1 package (5 ounces, or 142 g) frozen cookie dough bites

1 package (5 ounces, or 142 g) frozen brownie batter bites

INSTRUCTIONS

1. I used a 24-inch (61-cm) rectangular board for serving. Pick one with a bit of a bowl shape or higher sides to help contain the ice that keeps your treats frozen.
2. Fill the platter with crushed ice or shaved ice. We used snow for this photo!
3. Arrange half the cookie sandwiches in a diagonal from corner to corner. Place the ice cream sandwiches on their sides so guests can easily see what's inside. Alternate the types of cookie sandwiches, wedging them into the ice to hold in place.
4. Arrange the remaining ice cream sandwiches above and below the line of cookie sandwiches.
5. Sprinkle the cookie dough and brownie batter bites at the ends of the cookie sandwich line.
6. Serve immediately or store the platter in the freezer until ready to serve.

Note: If you don't have crushed ice or freshly fallen snow, place your ice in a large, heavy-duty bag and smash with a mallet or rolling pin. You can do this step up to a week in advance. Store your crushed ice in the freezer in a bag until ready to use.

Cookie Decorating BOARD

Serves 10. Have fun decorating cookies any time of year with a cookie decorating board! Basic sugar cookie cutouts in a variety of shapes are arranged on a large sheet pan along with everything you need to decorate your own cookies. Frosting, sprinkles, candy, and even candy eyes make this a fun activity for kids young and old. The baking sheet contains some of the mess and makes cleanup a breeze. It's perfect for holiday parties, too, to keep little hands busy!

INGREDIENTS

Homemade Treats

12 Basic Sugar Cookies
(page 131)

Store-Bought Sweets

1 cup (192 g) rainbow sprinkles

1 cup (192 g) candy-coated
chocolate sprinkles

1 cup (192 g) sweet tart
sprinkles

¼ cup (48 g) chocolate
sprinkles

¼ cup (48 g) green sprinkles

¼ cup (48 g) red sprinkles

¼ cup (48 g) candy eyes

¼ cup (44 g) mini chocolate
chips

2 cups (250 g) chocolate
frosting

2 cups (250 g) vanilla frosting

2 cups (250 g) strawberry
frosting

INSTRUCTIONS

1. I used a half-sheet pan for serving.
2. Arrange six different-size bowls on the right side of the sheet pan and fill each with one type of sprinkles.
3. Arrange the cookies on the other side of the board.
4. Fill the spaces in between the bowls with the candy eyes and mini chocolate chips.
5. Fill a pastry bag fitted with a decorating tip with the chocolate frosting. Fill an additional 2 pastry bags with the vanilla and strawberry frosting.
6. Place the pastry bags on the edges of the sheet pan and serve.

Note: You can make a larger platter for a bigger crowd and add more cookies as needed. If you don't have a pastry bag or prefer not to buy them, a regular zip-top bag works well. Just fill the bag with the frosting and snip off one corner with a pair of scissors. Pipe the frosting onto the cookies with the bag.

After-School Sweets BOARD

Serves 3. Sweets after school—but make it healthy and fun! Fruit skewers and marshmallow fruit dip are the perfect centerpiece for these individual after-school sweets boards. Mini slate boards are filled with simple fruit skewers, fruit-and-nut bar bites, roasted nuts, animal crackers, and a mini muffin. Kids LOVE having their very own board to snack on when they arrive home from school, and this spread ensures they're fueling up with good-for-you sweets.

INGREDIENTS

Homemade Treats
½ cup (48 g) Marshmallow
    Fruit Dip (page 136)

Store-Bought Sweets
3 fruit skewers (use any fruit
    your kids love and thread on
    a bamboo skewer)
1 fruit-and-nut bar, cut into
    thirds
¼ cup (36 g) salted, roasted
    peanuts
9 animal crackers
3 mini muffins, any flavor

INSTRUCTIONS

1. I used three 6-inch (15-cm) slate boards for serving.
2. Assemble the fruit skewers with your children's favorite fruit. We used strawberries, assorted berries, bananas, and grapes for our fruit skewers.
3. Fill a small bowl with 2 to 3 tablespoons (15 g) of fruit dip and top with a halved strawberry. Place the bowl on a corner of the board.
4. Arrange the skewer in the center of the board and scatter the remaining items around the skewer.
5. Serve immediately.

Note: If you prefer not to use marshmallow fruit dip, you can fill the bowls with yogurt for dipping instead. Also, for a nut-free option, use sunflower seeds instead of peanuts and a kids protein bar that's nut-free as a substitute for the fruit-and-nut bar.

Kids' Sugar Rush BOARD

Serves 12. The ultimate kids fantasy sweets board! The sugar rush board was dreamed up by my kids with everything they'd ever want on their very own dessert board. From giant rainbow swirl lollipops to birthday cake caramel corn, this fun board has everything a kid or kid at heart could want. Candy, cookies, chocolate . . . the sky's the limit with this one. Perfect for a kid's birthday party or to celebrate the last day of school!

INGREDIENTS

Homemade Treats
12 Chocolate-Covered Pretzels (page 136)

Store-Bought Sweets
½ cup (104 g) sweet tarts candy

½ cups (120 g) Nerds candy

3–6 swirl rainbow lollipops (more if you're having a crowd)

8 ounces (225 g) frosted animal crackers

12 chocolate chip cookies

8 ounces (225 g) red licorice twists

12 fudge stripe cookies

4 cups (47 g) cotton candy

3 cups (128 g) birthday cake caramel corn or regular caramel corn

1 cup (150 g) gummy candy watermelon

INSTRUCTIONS

1. I used a 24-inch (61-cm) round board for serving.
2. Place two small ramekins or bowls on each side of the board. Fill one bowl with the sweet tarts and one bowl with the Nerds.
3. Place the lollipops at the top center of the board and shingle them down to the center of the board.
4. Arrange the animal crackers to the left of the lollipops in a group, then shingle the chocolate chip cookies to the left of the animal crackers.
5. Place the pretzels on the bottom left of the board, then add the licorice at the top of the board directly across from the pretzels.
6. Arrange the fudge stripe cookies across from the chocolate chip cookies.
7. Fluff up the cotton candy and place it in the space above the fudge stripe cookies.
8. Add the caramel corn and watermelon slices at the bottom of the board.

Note: This board can be assembled a few hours in advance. Add the cotton candy right before serving; moisture or humidity can cause it to shrink up if left out too long.

5

Celebration

BOARDS

Wedding Cake BOARD

Serves 12. Perfect for a smaller ceremony, this wedding cake board is simple and sweet. A mini tiered wedding cake is the centerpiece, with coordinating cupcakes and petit fours, champagne gummy bears, champagne gumdrops, macarons, and chocolates. They frame the cake beautifully so there's a little something for everyone to enjoy. Enlist the help of your favorite bakery to make the tiered wedding cake with the coordinating cupcakes and petit fours.

INGREDIENTS

Store-Bought Sweets

1 12-inch (30-cm) tiered wedding cake

12 mini cupcakes

6–8 petit fours

12 chocolate-dipped assorted cookies

12 assorted chocolate truffles

1½ cups (270 g) champagne gummy bears

1½ cups (273 g) champagne gumdrops

12 assorted macarons

Mini chocolate champagne bottles

INSTRUCTIONS

1. I used a 24-inch (61-cm) round board for serving.
2. Place the cake at the top center of the board, being sure to leave a few inches at the top of the board.
3. Place the cupcakes to the right of the cake, then arrange the petit fours to the left.
4. Fill the space above the cake with the chocolate-dipped cookies. Essentially, you're using the ingredients to cover the cake board your bakery will build the cake on.
5. Arrange the remaining ingredients in clusters or groups around the cake, filling in the spaces to ensure most of the board is covered.
6. To serve, you may need to remove the treats from the board before cutting the cake and serving.

Note: Order extra cupcakes, petit fours, and macarons to replenish the board as needed and to fill the area where the cake has been if it's removed to cut for serving. This will ensure you still have a beautiful board even when the cake has been taken away.

Game Day Sweets BOARD

Serves 12. Score with the ultimate game day sweets board! It has everything you need to keep you sugared up during the big game, starting with a ball-shaped brownie! We didn't stop there . . . we even made mini chocolate-covered strawberries with laces, piped laces on a few chocolate-covered almonds, and decorated our crispy cereal treats like artificial turf. Cupcakes, mini and standard size, are also decorated with a festive spin. Your local bakery can easily make any of the items on this board, or you can make your own.

INGREDIENTS

Homemade Treats

1 Ball Brownie (1 recipe Fudge Brownies, page 129, cut into the shape of a ball)

8 Chocolate-Covered Strawberries (page 129)

12 Chocolate-Covered Pretzels (page 136)

12 Crispy Cereal Treats (page 130; with green frosting and piped with a yard line)

Semi-Homemade Sweets

1 cup (121 g) chocolate-covered almonds

White and green frosting, for decorating

Store-Bought Sweets

6 mini cupcakes

6 standard cupcakes with green frosting

1 cup (227 g) green and white starburst candies

INSTRUCTIONS

1. I used a 24-inch (61-cm) rectangle wood tray for serving.
2. To make the ball, bake the brownies according to the instructions and, once cooled, cut into the shape of a ball. Decorate using green and white frosting, as desired.
3. Place the ball in the middle of the tray.
4. Pipe the laces onto the strawberries and almonds using white frosting in a piping bag. Allow to set.
5. Arrange the crispy cereal treats at the top left of the ball and the strawberries on the opposite side of the tray.
6. Place the pretzels in the bottom-left corner and fill the space between the pretzels and crispy cereal treats with the almonds.
7. Be sure the decorated almonds are on the top of the pile if you didn't decorate them all.
8. Arrange the cupcakes in the bottom-right corner of the board and fill the remaining space with the starburst candies.

Note: The brownie can be made up to 24 hours in advance and stored at room temperature, covered, until ready to serve.

Birthday Confetti BOARD

Serves 18. Celebrate your next birthday with an overload of sprinkles and confetti on the birthday confetti board! Everything you need for the sweetest party ever, sprinkle-coated treats surround a mini birthday cake that's deliciously festive. With mini donuts, nonpareils, frosted animal crackers, pretzels, funfetti crispy cereal treats, birthday cake caramel corn, macarons, and more, this colorful board will put a smile on everyone's face.

INGREDIENTS

Homemade Treats
12 Chocolate-Covered Pretzels
 (page 136)
8 funfetti Crispy Cereal Treats
 (page 130)

Store-Bought Sweets
1 6-inch (15-cm) single-layer
 birthday cake
8 ounces (225 g) frosted
 animal crackers
1 package (8 ounces, or 225 g)
 pastel nonpareils
6 assorted macarons
6 mini rainbow-sprinkle donuts
2 cups (85 g) birthday cake
 caramel corn
6 mini or 3 standard cupcakes
 decorated with sprinkles
10 chocolate sandwich cookies
8 mini rainbow swirl lollipops
Sprinkles or small candies,
 such as sweet tarts

INSTRUCTIONS

1. I used a 24-inch (61-cm) round board for serving.
2. Place the cake in the center of the board.
3. Arrange the animal crackers at the top of the cake, fanning them out to form a small triangle.
4. Repeat the process by adding the nonpareils and half of the pretzels to the left of the animal crackers.
5. Place the macarons in a row standing on their sides so they're easier to grab.
6. Pile the mini donuts next to the macarons—this will help keep them from rolling.
7. Arrange the cupcakes about 4 to 6 inches (10 to 15 cm) over from the donuts, and fill the gap with the caramel corn.
8. Position the remaining pretzels directly across from the arranged pretzels in the same fashion.
9. Arrange the sandwich cookies in a row on their sides, similar to the macarons. Place the lollipops next to them.
10. Fill the remaining board space with the crispy cereal treats.
11. Fill any additional gaps on your board with sprinkles or another small treat.

Awards Night BOARD

Serves 3. Whether it's the Oscars, the Golden Globes, or Miss Universe, this awards night board will make you feel like you're just as glamorous as the nominees. Simple yet decadent, this dessert board is embellished with rich crème brûlée, mini opera cakes, and champagne gummy candy. Serve with a bottle of bubbly and float away to Lala Land.

INGREDIENTS

Store-Bought Sweets

3 mini crème brûlée bowls (you can find them at most well-stocked grocery stores or pastry shops)

1 cup (150 g) assorted fresh berries

6 mini opera cakes

1 cup (270 g) champagne gummy bears

1 cup (273 g) champagne gumdrops

6 pieces artisan chocolate

INSTRUCTIONS

1. I used a 14-inch (36-cm) rectangular marble board for serving.
2. Arrange the crème brûlée in a zigzag pattern on the board and garnish with fresh berries.
3. Position the opera cakes on their sides around the board.
4. Fill in the remaining spaces with the gummy bears and gumdrops.
5. Garnish with the chocolates, and serve immediately.

Note: If you can't find crème brûlée at the store, call your favorite restaurant and ask if you can order it to go. You may need to create the brûlée topping at home before serving, but that's simple to do with a kitchen torch and a sprinkle of sugar.

6

Any Time

BOARDS

Chocolate and Truffles BOARD

Serves 8. A chocolate lover's heaven on a board . . . every shape, size, and flavor chocolate you can find works perfectly on this chocolate and truffles board. Artisan truffles in an assortment of sizes and flavors are paired perfectly with grocery store chocolates for the perfect balance of decadence. Serve this at your next girls' night, book club meeting, or small celebration.

INGREDIENTS

Store-Bought Sweets

16 assorted large artisan chocolate truffles

16 mini cupcake wrappers (optional)

8 ounces (225 g) chocolate bark

9 assorted small artisan chocolate truffles

1 box assorted chocolates (12 chocolates or more)

INSTRUCTIONS

1. I used a 24-inch (61-cm) rectangle board for serving.
2. Place the large truffles in the cupcake wrappers (if using) and arrange them on the board in any pattern you like.
3. Break up the chocolate bark and add it to a small corner of the board in a stack.
4. Fill in the remaining areas of the board with the mini truffles and assorted chocolates.

Note: You can skip the chocolate bark and add more truffles, if you prefer. The mix of assorted chocolates, small truffles, and chocolate bark allows you to build a bigger board without breaking the bank.

Chocolate-Covered Everything BOARD

Serves 6. Dip everything in chocolate and call it dessert! This chocolate-covered everything board is so simple and unassuming, but there's never a morsel left. There are no rules here—you can dip almost anything you want in chocolate and call it dessert. We went with marshmallows, strawberries, apple slices, cookies, apricots, and potato chips. Don't skip the chips . . . they're insanely amazing. All the ingredients are semi-homemade, but it takes about 15 minutes from start to finish.

INGREDIENTS

Semi-Homemade Sweets

8 ounces (225 g) chocolate melting wafers

6 large marshmallows

6 strawberries

1 granny smith apple, cut into wedges

6 fudge stripe cookies

6 or more potato chips (they will vanish quickly!)

6–8 dried apricots

INSTRUCTIONS

1. I used a 24-inch (61-cm) rectangular board for serving.
2. Melt the chocolate in a microwave-safe bowl at high power for 30 seconds. Stir and repeat at 30-second increments until the chocolate is melted and smooth.
3. Line a baking sheet with parchment paper and dip all the ingredients into the chocolate to coat. You can dip them all the way in if you prefer, but I like how they look half-dipped.
4. Allow the chocolate to set before arranging on the board.
5. Add the marshmallows to the top-right corner in a cluster, then arrange three strawberries to the right of the marshmallows.
6. Place the apple slices below the marshmallows in a small group, then shingle the potato chips down the right side of the board.
7. Add the cookies to the board below the apples, then place the remaining strawberries below the chips.
8. Arrange the apricots at the bottom of the board and serve.

Note: Chocolate melting wafers are round chocolate disks that are made for melting and candy making. You can find them at most well-stocked grocery stores in the baking aisle. If you can't find melting chocolate wafers, you can use a chocolate baking bar chopped into small pieces. Melt in the microwave as directed or use a double boiler.

Brownies and Bars
BOARD

Serves 12. Who doesn't love a brownie . . . or a bar cookie? Brownies, bars, and bar-like treats come in all shapes and sizes with this brownie and bar board. Brownie bites are the centerpiece but don't overshadow all the other goodies that make up this mouthwatering display. Lemon bars, magic bars, streusel bars, crispy cereal treats, chocolate chip cookie bars, and layered brownies definitely can hold their own here. The only problem . . . how to choose which to eat first.

INGREDIENTS

Semi-Homemade Sweets
4 Epic Layered Brownies
   (see note)
4 funfetti Crispy Cereal Treats
   (page 130)

Store-Bought Sweets
24 mini brownie bites
4 magic bars
4 lemon bars
4 raspberry streusel bars
9 chocolate chip cookie bars

INSTRUCTIONS

1. I used a 20-inch (51-cm) round board for serving.
2. Arrange the brownie bites down the center of the board.
3. Place the magic bars in a pile to the left of the brownie river. Arrange the lemon bars below the magic bars and then the streusel bars in a group below the lemon bars.
4. To the right of the brownie river, arrange the layered brownies and chocolate chip cookie bars in a group.
5. Below the layered brownies, arrange the funfetti crispy treats. Serve.

Note: To make the layered brownies, buy premade brownies at the store and top with 2 tablespoons (32 g) creamy peanut butter. Allow the peanut butter to firm up in the refrigerator and then top with store-bought cookie dough. (Look for edible cookie dough in tubs in the refrigerated cookie dough section of the grocery store.) Top with a spoonful of hot fudge sauce. Allow to set for 1 hour then serve. You can make these up to 2 days in advance. Store in the refrigerator in an airtight container until ready to serve.

Sweet Summer Fruit Salad BOARD

Serves 8. A refreshingly sweet treat for hot summer days, this summer fruit salad board is overflowing with fresh fruit, sweet macarons, and berry pound cake kabobs. Add a few chocolate-covered strawberries for the ultimate dessert. Serve with whipped cream for topping and dipping!

INGREDIENTS
Store-Bought Sweets

1 pineapple
2 cups (300 g) diced watermelon
1 cup (145 g) blueberries
1 cup (125 g) raspberries
1½ cups (220 g) blackberries (reserve 8 berries for the skewers)
1 cup (178 g) sliced kiwi fruit
1 pint (357 g) strawberries, rinsed and hulled
1 pound cake, cut into 1-inch (2.5-cm) cubes
8 skewers
8 mini waffle bowls
1 cup (60 g) whipped cream
4–8 chocolate-covered strawberries
8 macarons
1 cup (140 g) fruit-and-nut trail mix

INSTRUCTIONS

1. I used a 24-inch (61-cm) round board for serving.
2. Cut the pineapple in half and scoop out the inside. Dice the pineapple into bite-size pieces.
3. Place the pineapple, watermelon, blueberries, raspberries, blackberries, and kiwi fruit in a large bowl. Toss to combine.
4. Arrange the pineapple at the top-right side of the board, cut-side up. Fill the pineapple with the fruit salad, reserving 1½ cups (378 g) and let it spill over the side to form a fruit salad river to the bottom of the board.
5. Thread the strawberries, pound cake, and one blackberry onto eight 6-inch (15-cm) bamboo skewers and arrange on the side of the board in a small pile.
6. Arrange the waffle bowls on the left side of the board and fill each with a large spoonful of the remaining fruit salad.
7. Fill a small bowl with whipped cream and place it to the left top of the pineapple.
8. Place the chocolate-covered strawberries along the top-right edge of the board.
9. Scatter the macarons and the trail mix in the empty areas of the board.
10. Serve immediately.

Note: To add more texture, sprinkle shredded coconut, chia seeds, or sliced almonds on top of the fruit salad.

Pie Love BOARD

Serves 6. When you can't decide between cherry or apple . . . or chocolate cream or pecan . . . serve them all on this epic pie board! We love pie, and when we couldn't decide which we should serve at our last gathering, this pie love board was born. It's simple, uncluttered, and served up with a big bowl of whipped cream, as all pie should be. You can make your own pie to showcase in the center of the board, or just purchase from your favorite bakery to make entertaining that much breezier. The slices are frozen, thawed pies from my grocer's freezer section. How easy is that?

INGREDIENTS

Store-Bought Sweets

1 large cherry crumb pie

2 mini apple crumb pies

1 mini chocolate cream pie

1 mini pecan pie

1 mini chocolate peanut
   butter pie

2 slices frozen, thawed
   chocolate silk pie

2 slices frozen, thawed key
   lime pie

3 cups (180 g) whipped cream
   or store-bought whipped
   topping

INSTRUCTIONS

1. I used a 24-inch (61-cm) round board for serving.
2. Carefully cut the cherry pie into six equal slices and arrange in the center of the board.
3. Place the mini pies around the larger pie.
4. Fill a bowl with the whipped cream and place at the bottom of the board.
5. Arrange the pie slices in the remaining area at the bottom of the board and serve.

Note: To make slicing your pies easier, cut the pie while chilled and wipe the knife clean after each cut.

Big Bundt Cake BOARD

Serves 20. I like big Bundts . . . and little Bundts and every flavor Bundt. Guests will LOVE the variety of the big Bundt cake board—which is made easy with bakery Bundt cakes. Use an assortment of flavors and sizes with one large Bundt cake cut into slices for those traditional Bundt lovers.

INGREDIENTS

Store-Bought Sweets

1 large marble Bundt cake, cut into 1-inch (2.5-cm) slices

6 medium assorted Bundt cakes

12 mini assorted Bundt cakes

Assorted fresh berries

INSTRUCTIONS

1. I used a 24-inch (61-cm) round board for serving.
2. Arrange the Bundt cake slices down the center of the board.
3. Place three of the medium Bundt cakes on each side of the board.
4. Position the remaining mini Bundt cakes in the open areas of the board.
5. Top all the cakes with a berry or two, as garnish.

Note: You may have noticed that I don't overload the cake and pie boards. The reason: it's easier to serve the cakes without breaking them into pieces. Because the cakes are softer and moist, they will fall apart if you have to dig around in between tons of other ingredients to serve them. If you want a fuller board, add fresh berries or nuts, or add sprinkles for color.

Ice Cream Sundae BOARD

Serves 8 to 10. Every day can be Sundae with an ice cream sundae board. This is a creative way to let guests DIY their own desserts: just add pints of ice cream nestled in a tray filled with ice alongside a second tray with an array of toppings. Serve everything with mini waffle bowls to keep cleanup minimal.

INGREDIENTS

Store-Bought Sweets

1 cup (175 g) mini chocolate chips

1 cup (122 g) granola

1 cup (192 g) rainbow sprinkles

1 cup (235 ml) hot fudge sauce

1 cup (175 g) butterscotch chips

½ cup (96 g) rainbow candy-coated sprinkles

½ cup (112 g) mini candy-coated chocolates

3 cups (180 g) whipped topping

10 mini waffle bowls

10 chocolate-dipped cookie straws

10 mini stroopwafels or other mini cookie

1 pint chocolate ice cream

1 pint vanilla ice cream

1 pint mint chocolate chip ice cream

INSTRUCTIONS

1. I used a 30-inch (76-cm) oval board for serving.
2. Place a baking dish in the center of the board. Do not fill with ice until ready to serve.
3. Arrange 8 small bowls or ramekins around the outside of the baking dish and fill each with the chocolate chips, granola, rainbow sprinkles, hot fudge sauce, butterscotch chips, sprinkles, chocolates, and whipped cream.
4. Stack the waffle bowls in a corner of the board and arrange the cookies in the remaining spaces around the board.
5. Right before serving, fill the baking dish with crushed or shaved ice.
6. Nestle the pints of ice cream deep into the ice so it's almost all the way up the sides. This will help keep them from melting too quickly.
7. Serve immediately with ice cream scoops for serving and spoons for eating.

Note: To prep ahead, fill the baking dish with ice and put the ice cream containers in to create a mold for each pint. Remove the pints and return them to the freezer. Put the entire baking dish filled with ice in the freezer until ready to serve. Arrange the board beforehand and just add the baking dish right before serving.

Cake and Cupcake BOARD

Serves 18. Elegant and simple, this cake and cupcake board is party-perfect and easy to pull together quickly with your favorite cake recipe or bakery classic. Vanilla, chocolate, and red velvet cakes are displayed with mini cupcakes in between. Serving is a breeze because the cake is already partially sliced, but you can still see the beauty of the decorating by keeping part of the cake intact.

INGREDIENTS

Store-Bought Sweets

1 vanilla cake, half the
   cake sliced

1 chocolate cake, half the
   cake sliced

1 red velvet cake, half the cake
   sliced

5 mini vanilla cupcakes

5 mini chocolate cupcakes

5 mini red velvet cupcakes

INSTRUCTIONS

1. I used a 24-inch (61-cm) round board for serving.
2. Slice half the vanilla cake and place one full cake wedge at the center of the board. Shingle a few slices beneath the cake wedge, leaving enough space between the wedge and the slices for the mini cupcakes.
3. Repeat with the chocolate cake and the red velvet cake.
4. Arrange the mini cupcakes within the space between the respective full cake wedges and its slices, and serve.

Note: You can serve any flavor cake you like using this method. Those with dietary preferences such as gluten-free or vegan or those with food allergies love when cakes are served separately using this cake display.

Picnic in the Park BOARD

Serves 2. Take your boards to the park for a cozy picnic for two. Apple turnovers, fruit, nuts, cookies, cheese, and macarons are simple to transport and assemble on a warm spring or summer day. This is the perfect impromptu date or simple snacks for friends. A glass of bubbly goes well with this simple board.

INGREDIENTS
Store-Bought Sweets

2 frozen apple turnovers

2 small bunches green seedless grapes

4 small wedges asiago cheese

1 cup (150 g) assorted fresh berries

4 chocolate-covered biscuits

4 white-chocolate-dipped biscuits

4 assorted macarons

¼ cup (28 g) candied walnuts

INSTRUCTIONS

1. I used two 6-inch (15-cm) wood boards for serving.
2. Bake the turnovers according to the package directions and cool to room temperature.
3. Cut the turnovers in half and arrange on one corner of the board.
4. Place one bunch of grapes on each board and position the cheese wedges in the center of each board.
5. Arrange the remaining ingredients on the board and serve.

Note: Feel free to substitute with your favorite cheese. You can find many varieties of individually wrapped cheeses in single serving sizes at most grocery stores.

Cheesecake BOARD

Serves 6. The perfect ending to a dinner party with friends, this cheesecake board offers something for everyone. Your local bakery will have everything you need without you even having to turn on the oven. We used personal-size cheesecakes in carrot, chocolate, and vanilla then added slices of plain cheesecake as well as marble. This board is as beautiful as it is delicious.

INGREDIENTS

Store-Bought Sweets

6 assorted mini personal-size cheesecakes

5 slices assorted cheesecake

Assorted fresh berries

INSTRUCTIONS

1. I used a 12-inch (30-cm) square ceramic platter for serving.
2. Arrange the personal cheesecakes in a row at the top and bottom of the board.
3. Position the slices, alternating, between the two rows of personal cheesecakes.
4. Top the cheesecake slices with berries as a garnish and serve.

Note: Assemble the board before guests arrive and store in the refrigerator until ready to serve. Most purchased cheesecakes can be stored, chilled, for up to 24 hours.

DIY Pudding Bar
BOARD

Serves 4. Weeknight dessert just became even more creative with a DIY pudding bar board. Simple bowls of pudding are served up with a variety of toppings so each person can make their own fun recipe. Serve the puddings of choice in individual bowls so everyone can just grab a bowl and sprinkle with nuts, drizzle with caramel, or top with berries. Serve with cookies and biscotti for crunch!

INGREDIENTS
Store-Bought Sweets

2 cups (568 g) assorted flavors premade pudding

¼ cup (60 ml) caramel sauce

¼ cup (30 g) chopped walnuts

¼ cup (48 g) sprinkles

4 stroopwafels

4 biscotti

1 cup (150 g) assorted fresh berries

4 chocolate-dipped cookie straws

INSTRUCTIONS
1. I used a 20-inch (51-cm) rectangle marble board for serving.
2. Scoop the pudding into individual bowls and arrange on the board.
3. Fill small serving bowls with the sauce, nuts, and sprinkles. Place on the board.
4. Arrange the remaining ingredients around the pudding dishes and serve.

Note: Prep ahead by filling the individual bowls with pudding and chilling in the refrigerator until ready to serve. This is a fantastic way to enjoy family movie night or a casual dinner party.

Chocolate Dipping BOARD

Serves 6. Healthy, crunchy, juicy, sweet, salty . . . everything goes with chocolate. That's what makes this chocolate dipping board so fantastically amazing. Every texture and flavor, savory or sweet, is loaded on this board with one beautiful bowl of chocolate sauce just waiting to be dunked into. Serve this one for just about any occasion, big or small.

INGREDIENTS

Store-Bought Sweets

2 cups (475 ml) chocolate dipping sauce

6 chocolate-dipped biscotti

12 mini biscotti

24 mini stroopwafels

8 figs, cut in half

3 oranges, peeled and segmented

2 pints (714 g) strawberries

1 pint (290 g) blueberries

INSTRUCTIONS

1. I used a 24-inch (61-cm) round board for serving.
2. Fill a serving bowl with the chocolate dipping sauce, and place it in the center of the board.
3. Arrange the biscotti and stroopwafels on the board first.
4. Fill the remaining areas of the board with the fruit, keeping each type of fruit together, and serve.

Note: Chocolate dipping sauce is usually in the produce section of the grocery store with the caramel apple dips or other fruit dips.

Chocolate and Cheese Pairing BOARD

Serves 8. Host a fun evening with friends with this chocolate and cheese pairing board. There's no better conversation than discussing which cheese goes best with what chocolate. Blue cheese, Brie, Gruyère, and taleggio were used to build this board, but try your favorite cheeses and load it up with chocolate. Both dark and milk chocolate are recommended for your pairing experience—and don't forget a few truffles and chocolate-covered almonds, too.

INGREDIENTS

Store-Bought Sweets

1 4-inch (10-cm) Brie wheel (we topped ours with a caramel pecan topping)

1 wedge blue cheese (Gorgonzola or Stilton are our go-tos)

5 ounces (142 g) Gruyère, sliced

5 ounces (142 g) taleggio, sliced

6 ounces (168 g) chocolate-covered almonds

5 ounces (142 g) milk chocolate bark

5 ounces (142 g) dark chocolate bark

8 small chocolate truffles

Raspberries (optional)

INSTRUCTIONS

1. I used a 12-inch (30-cm) round wood board for serving.
2. Arrange the cheese on the board in a square shape (four corners) and fan out the sliced cheese.
3. Using a cheese knife or spreader, break up some of the blue cheese for easy serving and to encourage guests to dig in.
4. Place the chocolate around the board in groups, and scatter the truffles around the board to fill in some of the gaps.
5. Garnish with the raspberries (if using) and serve.

Note: Before serving the board, leave the cheese at room temperature for 1 hour. This will enhance the flavor of the cheese.

Ultimate Cookie BOARD

Serves 12 to 14. Cookies and milk has never been a better snack than when you're noshing on the ultimate cookie board. A variety of classic cookies dipped in chocolate and sprinkled with sugar are perfect for dunking in glasses of milk. Use your own cookie recipes or make things easy and pick up an assortment of bakery favorites.

INGREDIENTS

Homemade Treats

12 Classic Chocolate Chip Cookies (page 132; half dipped in chocolate)

Store-Bought Sweets

8 sugar cookies

4 white chocolate cranberry cookies

4 chocolate rugelach

4 fruit-filled rugelach

4 pecan sandies

4 chocolate-dipped shortbread cookies

Milk, for serving

INSTRUCTIONS

1. I used a large 24-inch (61-cm) round board, which is the perfect size for serving 12 to 14 people. You can use a smaller board if you're serving fewer people.
2. Arrange the sugar cookies and chocolate cranberry cookies in a shingled arrangement, forming a circle around the outside of the board. Group the cookies together as you form the circle to keep the look uniform.
3. Add the rugelach, pecan sandies, and shortbread cookies grouped together in small mounds in the center of the circle.
4. Serve with milk in smaller juice glasses or shot glasses!

Note: Extra cookies are fun to serve alongside in smaller ramekins.

S'mores BOARD

Serves 12. Light the campfire and build the ultimate s'mores board for the best summer memories. (And the tastiest, too!) Overflowing with everything you need to build the most amazing s'mores ever, this board has cookies, crackers, candy, chocolate hazelnut spread, dulce de leche, peanut butter, nonpareils, and pretzels! A little salty, a little sweet . . . you can literally have it your way.

INGREDIENTS

Homemade Treats
4 Classic Chocolate Chip Cookies (page 132)

Store-Bought Sweets
1 cup (260 g) chocolate hazelnut spread
1 cup (260 g) peanut butter
1 cup (235 ml) dulce de leche
1 cup (175 g) mini nonpareils
4 chocolate oatmeal cookies
4 sugar cookies
8 large graham crackers, broken in half
16 round crackers
24 pretzel crisps
12 mini chocolate chip cookies
8 peanut butter cups
6 chocolate bars, broken in half
6 jumbo marshmallows
24 regular marshmallows

INSTRUCTIONS

1. I used a 24-inch (61-cm) round board for serving.
2. Fill serving bowls with the chocolate hazelnut spread, peanut butter, dulce de leche, and nonpareils. Place the bowls on the board.
3. Arrange the cookies down the center of the board, and fan the crackers around the edges of the board.
4. Fill the center of the board with the pretzels, mini cookies, peanut butter cups, chocolate, and marshmallows.
5. Add spoons or spreaders to the bowls for serving.

Note: Serve the bowl with clean sticks or long skewers for tasting marshmallows. And napkins . . . lots of napkins.

Dessert for Two BOARD

Serves 2. Simple and sweet! Add a little sugar to your next date night with an assortment of chocolate desserts artfully arranged on a pretty platter. Cupcakes, fudge brownie bites, chocolates, and cookie dough bites are more than enough to satisfy your sweet tooth.

INGREDIENTS

Homemade Treats

2 Fudge Brownies (page 129)

Store-Bought Sweets

2 chocolate cupcakes

2 cookie dough truffles or your favorite chocolate truffles

6 assorted chocolates

INSTRUCTIONS

1. I used a small 12-inch (30-cm) platter for this board.
2. Arrange the cupcakes on opposite corners of the platter.
3. Place the truffles in the center on a diagonal to start to form a square.
4. Place the brownie bites to finish the corners of the square in the center of the board.
5. Arrange three chocolates on the opposite corners of the cupcakes, and finish with the remaining chocolates to balance the board.

Notes: If you have a larger board, you can decorate with flower petals or small rosebuds. Freeze the remaining brownies if you make a whole batch.

Hot Cocoa BOARD

Serves 14 to 18. Everyone loves a steaming cup of hot cocoa, but make it extra special with this easy board. Chocolate-covered marshmallows, peppermint spoons, chocolate-dipped pretzels, and a mini marshmallow river are just some of the things you can add to allow everyone to make their drinks completely customized. To keep the hot cocoa hot, serve it in a slow cooker with a ladle so guests can serve themselves.

INGREDIENTS

Homemade Treats
8–10 Chocolate-Covered Pretzels (pag 136)

Semi-Homemade Sweets
Chocolate-Dipped Marshmallows (page 94, Chocolate-Covered Everything Board)

Store-Bought Sweets
3 cups (150 g) mini marshmallows

½ cup (87 g) mini chocolate nonpareils

½ cup (87 g) mini mint nonpareils

½ cup (336 g) crushed peppermint candies

24 chocolate-covered sandwich cookies

2 cups (454 g) peppermint candies

24 chocolate-covered marshmallow toppers

Assorted cookies and chocolates

4–6 peppermint spoons

2 quarts (1.9 L) hot cocoa (serve more or less depending on the number of guests you're serving)

INSTRUCTIONS

1. I used a large 24-inch (61-cm) round board, which is the perfect size for serving 14 to 18 people. You can use a smaller board if you're serving fewer people.
2. Arrange the mini marshmallows down the center of the board to form the "river."
3. Place three small ramekins on the board in a triangle shape. We have two mugs on this board, but if you're serving a larger crowd, you can fill those spaces with more candy, chocolate chips, or bowls with caramel sauce. Let your creative juices flow!
4. Add the chocolate nonpareils, mint nonpareils, and crushed peppermint to the bowls.
5. Arrange the pretzels, cookies, and chocolate around the board in a fan shape. I like to shingle the flatter items such as the round chocolate-covered marshmallows and sandwich cookies to keep things tidy.
6. Fill in the spaces with the remaining candies, cookies, and chocolates.

Movie Night BOARD

Serves 8. Snacks are a MUST-HAVE for family movie night, and what better way to serve up a buffet of movie treats than on a board? To keep things contained, we upgrade our board to a tray with higher sides and arrange a few bowls to contain our favorite movie-theater candy. Fill the rest of the tray with popcorn and . . . action!

INGREDIENTS
Store-Bought Sweets

1 cup (208 g) sweet tart candies

1 cup (240 g) Nerds candy

1½ cups (270 g) gummy bears

1½ cups (132 g) chocolate-covered caramels

1½ cups (100 g) Junior Mints or other chocolate-covered peppermints

1 cup (175 g) mini chocolate nonpareils

4 cups (44 g) popcorn

INSTRUCTIONS

1. Arrange the bowls in a deep tray. I like to use one that's about 24 inches (61 cm) in length with sides that are approximately 3 inches (7.5 cm) deep to contain all the popcorn.
2. Fill each bowl with the candy.
3. Add the popcorn to the tray to fill in all the spaces between the bowls.
4. Serve!

Notes: If you want to butter and salt the popcorn, do this in a bowl before adding the popcorn to the tray.

7

RECIPES FOR

Homemade
Treats

Fudge Brownies

MAKES 12 BROWNIES

Ingredients

¾ cup (94 g) all-purpose flour

1 cup (86 g) unsweetened cocoa powder

1 teaspoon kosher salt

1½ cups (340 g, or 3 sticks) unsalted butter, cut into cubes

3 large eggs, at room temperature

1¾ cups (350 g) granulated sugar

1 teaspoon vanilla bean paste or pure vanilla extract

7 ounces (196 g) semisweet chocolate chunks

Instructions

1. Preheat the oven to 350°F (175°C, or gas mark 4).
2. Butter and flour a 9-inch (23-cm) square baking pan and set it aside.
3. In a large bowl, whisk together the flour, cocoa powder, and salt. Set aside.
4. In a small saucepan, melt half the butter over medium heat, stirring occasionally. Put the remaining butter in a medium bowl; pour the melted butter over top and stir to melt. The butter should look creamy but still have small pieces of unmelted butter throughout.
5. In the bowl of a stand mixer, mix the eggs and sugar on medium until thick and pale yellow. Add the vanilla, turn the mixer to low, and add one-third of the dry ingredients to the mixer. Stir in one-third of the butter. Continue alternating ingredients, stirring until combined. Add the chocolate and mix well.
6. Pour the batter into the prepared baking pan and spread evenly. Bake for 40 to 45 minutes, or until a cake tester inserted into the center comes out with a few crumbs sticking to it. Cool in the pan until the brownie is just a bit warmer than room temperature.
7. Run a knife around the edges of the brownie and invert onto a cutting board. Cut the brownie into twelve rectangles.

Chocolate-Covered Strawberries

MAKES 24 STRAWBERRIES

Ingredients

24 whole strawberries

10 ounces (280 g) good-quality dark or milk chocolate (if using bar chocolate, finely chop before melting)

5 ounces (142 g) good-quality white chocolate (optional)

Instructions

1. Rinse berries in cool water and dry thoroughly with a paper towel. Arrange in a single layer on a towel and allow to air-dry for 10 to 15 minutes, or until completely dry.
2. Line a baking sheet with parchment paper. Place the chocolate in a microwave-safe bowl and heat at high power for 30 seconds. Stir and heat in 30-second increments, until melted and smooth.
3. Dip the strawberries, one at a time, in the chocolate, turning to coat. Allow the excess to drip off and place the strawberry on the baking sheet. Push the strawberry forward ½ inch (1 cm) to help avoid the chocolate puddle from forming at the tip of the berry. Repeat with the remaining berries until all are coated.
4. Transfer the baking sheet to a cool, dry place to allow the chocolate to set.
5. If desired, melt white chocolate in 30-second increments in a microwave-safe bowl, then transfer the melted chocolate to a zip-top bag. Snip off a corner and drizzle over the strawberries.
6. Allow the chocolate to set.
7. Serve the strawberries immediately after they're set, or transfer to an airtight container lined with a paper towel (to absorb moisture) and refrigerate for up to 2 days.

Crispy Cereal Treats

MAKES 12 TREATS

Ingredients

6 cups (192 g) crispy rice cereal
5 tablespoons (69 g) salted butter
1 package (16 ounces, or 455 g) large
   marshmallows
2 cups (100 g) mini marshmallows
1 tablespoon (15 g) vanilla bean paste or pure
   vanilla extract

Instructions

1. Pour the cereal into a large mixing bowl. Set
   aside.
2. Over medium heat, add the butter to a large
   saucepan and melt.
3. Add the large marshmallows to the pot. Stir
   to combine with the butter. Continue to stir
   until the marshmallows have melted and are
   smooth.
4. Add the mini marshmallows to the pot and
   stir until they start to melt but are still visible.
5. Turn off the heat and stir in the vanilla bean
   paste.
6. Pour the marshmallow mixture over the
   cereal. Stir to combine.
7. Pour the cereal mixture into a 13 x 9–inch
   (33 x 23–cm) baking dish coated with cooking
   spray. Press the mixture into an even layer
   with your hands coated in butter or cooking
   spray to prevent sticking.
8. Allow the mixture to cool to room
   temperature. Cut the treats into
   approximately 3-inch (7.5-cm) squares and
   serve immediately, or transfer to an airtight
   container and store at room temperature for
   up to 5 days.

To create funfetti crispy treats:
Add ¾ cup (144 g) rainbow sprinkles to the
marshmallow mix right before pouring over the
crispy rice cereal. Fold to combine.

To create candy crispy treats:
Pour the marshmallow mixture over the crispy
rice cereal and then fold in 1 cup of candy.
Stir to combine.

To create frosted crispy treats:
Make the crispy treats as directed and allow to
set for 30 minutes. Using your favorite frosting
recipe or store-bought frosting, spread a layer
of frosting over the crispy treats before cutting.
Allow to stand for 30 minutes. Cut the crispy
treats into squares and decorate as desired.

Basic Sugar Cookies

MAKES 24 COOKIES

Ingredients

2½ cups (314 g) all-purpose flour
½ cup (65 g) cornstarch
¾ teaspoon baking powder
¼ teaspoon salt
1 cup (225 g) unsalted butter, cut into cubes and chilled
1 cup (200 g) granulated sugar
1 egg, lightly beaten with a whisk or fork
1 tablespoon (15 ml) milk
1 teaspoon vanilla extract
Powdered sugar, for rolling out dough

Instructions

1. Whisk together the flour, cornstarch, baking powder, and salt until combined. Set aside.
2. In the bowl of a stand mixer fitted with the paddle attachment, beat the butter and sugar until light and fluffy.
3. Turn the mixer to low and add the egg. Beat to combine.
4. Add the milk and vanilla, continuing to beat until well combined.
5. Slowly add the dry ingredients to the sugar mixture and beat until the dough begins to pull away from the sides.

For slice-and-bake cookies:

6. Divide the dough in half. Roll each half into a log approximately 2 inches (5 cm) in diameter. Wrap tightly in plastic wrap. Chill for 1 hour or up to 24 hours; the dough can be frozen at this point for up to 2 months.
7. When ready to bake, preheat the oven to 375°F (190°C, or gas mark 5). Line a baking sheet with parchment paper.
8. Slice the dough into ¼-inch (6-mm) rounds. Place the cookies on the baking sheet and bake for 6 to 8 minutes, until the edges are golden brown and the centers are set.
9. Transfer to a cooling rack and allow to cool to room temperature.

For cutout cookies:

6. Divide the dough into two equal disks and wrap tightly with plastic wrap.
7. Chill the dough for 1 hour or up to 24 hours; the dough can be frozen at this point for up to 2 months.
8. Preheat the oven to 375°F (190°C, or gas mark 5). Line a baking sheet with parchment paper. Sprinkle powdered sugar on a clean, dry surface and roll out one dough disk to ¼ inch (6 mm) thick.
9. Using a cookie cutter, cut out shapes and arrange them approximately 1 inch (2.5 cm) apart on the baking sheet.
10. Bake for 6 to 7 minutes, or until the cookies are just turning golden brown around the edges.
11. Allow the cookies to cool on the baking sheet for 1 to 2 minutes before transferring to a cooling rack to cool completely before decorating.
12. Repeat with the remaining dough.

Notes:
Baked cookies can be stored in an airtight container for up to 1 week at room temperature.

Basic Sugar Cookie Icing

MAKES ICING FOR 24 COOKIES

Ingredients
4 ounces (120 ml) pasteurized egg whites
1 teaspoon vanilla extract
4 cups (480 g) powdered sugar
Food coloring (optional)

Instructions
1. In the bowl of an electric mixer, mix the egg whites and vanilla until frothy.
2. Gradually add the sugar and mix on low speed until the sugar is incorporated and the icing is shiny. Turn the mixer to medium-high and beat for 5 to 7 minutes, until the mixture forms stiff, shiny peaks.
3. Stir in food coloring, if desired.
4. For immediate use, transfer the icing to a pastry bag fitted with a tip and pipe onto the cookies. Or if you're using a zip-top bag, clip the corner and pipe onto cookies.
5. Icing can be stored in an airtight container for up to 3 days.

Classic Chocolate Chip Cookies

MAKES 24 COOKIES

Ingredients
2¼ cups (282 g) all-purpose flour
1 teaspoon baking soda
1 teaspoon baking powder
1 teaspoon kosher salt
1 cup (225 g) salted butter, softened
1½ cups (300 g) granulated sugar
1 teaspoon vanilla bean paste
2 large eggs
1 cup (175 g) semisweet chocolate chips
1 cup (175 g) dark chocolate chips
½ cup (87 g) mini 70% dark chocolate chips

Instructions
1. Preheat the oven to 350°F (175°C, or gas mark 4). Line a baking sheet with parchment paper.
2. In a large bowl, whisk together the flour, baking soda, baking powder, and salt. Set aside.
3. In the bowl of an electric mixer, beat the butter and sugar until fluffy. Add the vanilla bean paste.
4. Add the eggs one at a time and mix thoroughly between each addition. Turn the mixer on low and slowly add the flour mixture. Turn off the mixer and fold in the chocolate chips.
5. Drop the dough by rounded tablespoonfuls onto the baking sheet. Bake for 9 to 11 minutes, or until golden brown. Transfer to a wire cooling rack, and store in an airtight container for up to 5 days.

Pound Cake

MAKES 1 POUND CAKE

Ingredients

1 cup (225 g) butter
1 cup (200 g) granulated sugar
4 large eggs
1 tablespoon (6 g) freshly grated lemon zest
1 teaspoon vanilla extract
1½ cups (188 g) all-purpose flour
½ teaspoon baking powder
¼ teaspoon kosher salt

Instructions

1. Preheat the oven to 350°F (175°C, or gas mark 4). Coat a 1-quart (1 L) loaf pan with cooking spray or lightly grease it with butter.
2. In the bowl of an electric mixer fitted with the paddle attachment, beat the butter on medium speed until fluffy.
3. Turn the mixer on low and slowly add the sugar to the butter. Beat until fluffy, approximately 2 to 3 minutes.
4. Add the eggs to the bowl one at a time, stopping to scrape down the sides of the bowl with a spatula. Add the lemon zest and vanilla, mixing on medium speed for 30 seconds longer to combine.
5. In a medium bowl, whisk together the flour, baking powder, and salt. Slowly add to the mixer on low speed. Stop to scrape down the sides of the bowl, then continue beating on low for 1 to 2 minutes.
6. Transfer the batter to the loaf pan.
7. Bake the cake for 1 hour, or until a toothpick inserted into the center of the cake comes out clean. Transfer to a wire rack to cool.
8. Once cooled, run a knife around the inside of the loaf pan to loosen the cake and turn out onto a platter to release.
9. Serve immediately or wrap tightly in plastic wrap and store at room temperature for up to 3 days.

Pound Cake French Toast

MAKES 8 SLICES

Ingredients

1 cup (235 ml) half-and-half
3 large eggs
1½ tablespoons (25 ml) maple syrup
1 teaspoon ground cinnamon
½ teaspoon vanilla extract
¼ teaspoon kosher salt
8 slices (½ inch, or 1 cm) pound cake (best if day old or older)
3 tablespoons (42 g) butter, divided
Powdered sugar, fruit, or maple syrup (optional)

Instructions

1. In a wide, shallow bowl (I like to use a pie plate), whisk together the half-and-half, eggs, syrup, cinnamon, vanilla, and salt.
2. Dip each cake slice in the egg mixture and allow to soak for 30 seconds on each side. Transfer to a baking sheet to allow the mixture to soak all the way through the cake.
3. Melt 2 tablespoons (28 g) of butter in a nonstick griddle pan over medium-high heat. Place four slices of the cake in the pan and cook for 2 to 3 minutes, until golden brown.
4. Carefully flip the cake over and continue cooking for 2 to 3 minutes, or until golden. Transfer to a platter and cover with foil to keep warm. Repeat with the remaining slices.
5. Serve immediately with powdered sugar, fruit, or maple syrup, if desired.

Blueberry Pancakes

SERVES 8

Ingredients

1½ cups (188 g) all-purpose flour
½ teaspoon kosher salt
2 teaspoons (9 g) baking powder
¾ teaspoon baking soda
½ tablespoon granulated sugar
½ tablespoon brown sugar
2¼ cups (530 ml) buttermilk
½ teaspoon vanilla extract
¼ cup (60 ml) melted butter, plus more
    for cooking
2 large eggs, lightly beaten with a fork or whisk
2 cups (290 g) fresh blueberries
Maple syrup, butter, and more fresh blueberries,
    for serving

Instructions

1. In a small bowl, whisk together the flour, salt, baking powder, baking soda, and both sugars until well combined.
2. In a separate larger bowl, whisk the buttermilk, vanilla, butter, and eggs until combined.
3. Fold in the dry ingredients until incorporated.
4. Heat a griddle or large nonstick skillet over medium-high heat. Add ½ tablespoon butter to the griddle and spread over the griddle to coat.
5. Add ¼ cup (60 ml) batter onto the griddle and sprinkle the batter evenly with a few of the blueberries.
6. Cook for 2 minutes, or until bubbles appear and the edges look dry, then flip and cook for 1 minute more. Your pancakes should be golden brown.
7. Repeat with the remaining batter and blueberries. Serve on your board or on a plate with maple syrup, butter, and fresh blueberries.

Vanilla Chia Seed Pudding

MAKES 2 CUPS (450 G)

Ingredients

1½ cups (355 ml) light coconut milk
3 tablespoons (33 g) chia seeds
1½ tablespoons (30 g) maple syrup
½ teaspoon vanilla extract

Instructions

1. Combine the coconut milk, chia seeds, maple syrup, and vanilla in a small bowl.
2. Cover and refrigerate for approximately 2 hours, or until the mixture has reached the consistency of pudding.
3. Store in an airtight container in the refrigerator for up to 3 days.

Cinnamon-Sugar Tortilla Chips

MAKES 80 CHIPS

Ingredients

½ cup (100 g) sugar
2 tablespoons (14 g) ground cinnamon
20 fresh corn tortillas, cut into quarters
Canola oil, for frying

Instructions

1. Heat about 1½ inches (3.5 cm) of oil in a large Dutch oven over medium heat until 350°F (175°C). Line a plate with several paper towels.
2. Whisk together the sugar and cinnamon in a small bowl.
3. Cooking in batches, add 3 to 4 tortilla pieces and fry for 1 to 2 minutes.
4. Flip the tortillas using tongs and fry for an additional 1 minute, or until they're golden brown and crisp.
5. Transfer to the lined plate.
6. Sprinkle the cinnamon-sugar immediately on the warm chips. Repeat until all the tortillas are fried and seasoned.
7. Store in an airtight container for up to 24 hours at room temperature.

Funnel Cake

MAKES 6 MEDIUM-SIZE FUNNEL CAKES

Ingredients

2 large eggs, room temperature
1½ cups (355 ml) milk
2 cups (250 g) all-purpose flour
1 teaspoon sugar
1 teaspoon baking powder
⅛ teaspoon salt
Canola oil, for frying
Powdered sugar (optional)

Instructions

1. Whisk together the eggs and milk in a large bowl. Set aside.
2. Stir together the flour, sugar, baking powder, and salt in a medium bowl.
3. Add the dry ingredients to the egg-milk mixture and whisk until smooth.
4. Line a plate with paper towels. Pour about 3 inches (7.5 cm) of oil into a large Dutch oven or heavy-duty pot.
5. Heat the oil over medium-high heat until the temperature reaches 375°F (190°C).
6. Using either a funnel or a measuring cup with a spout, pour the batter in a steady stream into the oil, starting from the center in a swirling motion to create a 6- to 7-inch (15- to 18-cm) round funnel cake.
7. Fry the funnel cake for 2 to 3 minutes, until golden brown. Flip and fry on the opposite side until golden and crispy.
8. Transfer to the lined plate and sprinkle with powdered sugar, if desired.

Marshmallow Fruit Dip

SERVES 8

Ingredients
8 ounces (225 g) marshmallow fluff
8 ounces (225 g) cream cheese, room
    temperature
1 teaspoon vanilla extract
Fresh fruit, for serving

Instructions
1. Place the marshmallow fluff, cream cheese
   and vanilla in a large bowl.
2. Beat the ingredients for 2 minutes, until
   smooth, light, and fluffy.
3. Transfer to a serving bowl, and serve with
   fresh fruit.

Chocolate-Covered Pretzels

MAKES 12 TO 14 PRETZELS

Ingredients
16 ounces (455 g) chopped chocolate or candy
    melts
12–14 pretzels
Assorted sprinkles, mini candy-coated
    chocolates, toffee chips, and chopped nuts

Instructions
1. Line a baking sheet with parchment paper.
2. Place the chocolate in a microwave-safe
   bowl and melt in the microwave at high
   power for 30 seconds. Stir and melt again
   in 30-second increments, stirring each time,
   until smooth.
3. Dip the pretzels into the melted chocolate,
   allowing the excess to drip off, and arrange
   on the baking sheet.
4. Sprinkle with your favorite toppings and
   allow to set for 20 to 30 minutes. Store in an
   airtight container until ready to serve.

Raspberry Jam

MAKES ABOUT 2 PINTS (940 ML)

Ingredients
1¾ cups (350 g) sugar
Juice and zest of 1 lemon
2 cups (340 g) fresh raspberries

Instructions
1. Add the sugar, lemon juice, and zest to a medium saucepan over low heat. Cook and stir until the sugar is completely dissolved.
2. Add the raspberries to the pan and continue to cook over low heat for 30 minutes, until the mixture is at a low boil. The mixture should be thickened a bit and almost the consistency of loose jam.
3. Remove from the heat and allow to cool for 15 minutes.
4. Transfer to two pint-size (475-ml) jars and seal with the lids. Store in the refrigerator for up to 2 weeks.

Acknowledgments

Writing your first book certainly comes with a learning curve, but writing a book during a pandemic throws another level of challenges you could never see coming. From quarantines to positive tests, we endured and made it through all the surprises and came out with a beautiful book at the end.

None of it would have been possible without a great team!

To Corinne, thank you just isn't enough for all the time, energy, love, creative juices, and photography expertise you offered during this book. I would not have been able to get this book completed without you. Your passion for photography shines through in every single shot.

Thank you, Dorothy, for sending Dan my way and for the opportunity to take on such a fun challenge. You're the most thoughtful and genuinely kind person. I'm so grateful I can call you my friend.

Chris, Katie, and Landon, thank you for being my biggest cheerleaders even when I had some rough days. Also, thank you for eating all the cookies, cakes, candy, cinnamon rolls, pancakes, and other goodies that I'd bring home every single day for weeks.

Thank you, Colleen, for your beautiful cake artistry and for creating some stunning centerpieces. You were able to take my crazy ideas and turn them into art. You are a master.

To the team at Quarto Books, thank you for the countless hours of work that went into making this book a reality. I learned so much along the way and am so thankful to have such a dedicated team.

About the Author

Kellie Hemmerly is the talented cook, writer, and photographer behind the popular blog *The Suburban Soapbox: A Good Life Tastes Great,* which focuses on family-friendly and healthy recipes, many of which are desserts, baking, and sweet creations. She has been a frequent contributor to NBC's "Today Food Club" at Today.com, and her work has been featured on the websites of *People* magazine and *Better Homes and Gardens,* among many others. She lives with her family near Philadelphia, Pennsylvania.

Index